MySpace

for Moms
and Dads

Also by Connie Neal

Dancing in the Arms of God

Connie Neal

MySpace

for Moms
and Dads

A Guide
to Understanding
the Risks
and the Rewards

ZONDERVAN®

ZONDERVAN.com/
AUTHORTRACKER
follow your favorite authors

MySpace for Moms and Dads
Copyright © 2007 by Connie Neal

Requests for information should be addressed to:
Zondervan, *Grand Rapids, Michigan* 49530

Library of Congress Cataloging-in-Publication Data

Neal, C. W. (Connie W.), 1958-
    MySpace for moms and dads : a guide to understanding the risks and the rewards / Connie
Neal.
        p. cm.
    Includes bibliographical references and indexes.
    ISBN-13: 978-0-310-27743-9
    ISBN-10: 0-310-27743-4
1. Myspace.com. 2. Internet and teenagers. 3. Online social networks. I. Title.
HQ799.2.I5 N43 2007

2006039554

Internet addresses (websites, blogs, etc.) and telephone numbers printed in this book are offered as a resource to you. These are not intended in any way to be or imply an endorsement on the part of Zondervan, nor do we vouch for the content of these sites and numbers for the life of this book.

Interior design by Beth Shagene
Illustration on page 16 by Casey Neal

Printed in the United States of America

07 08 09 10 11 12 13 14 15 • 24 23 22 21 20 19 18 17 16 15 14 13 12 11 10 9 8 7 6 5 4 3 2 1

Contents

Part 1
The MySpace Revolution

Part 2
Exploring MySpace:
An Introduction to the Site

Part 3
How Teens Use MySpace

Part 4
Parental Decisions about MySpace

Acknowledgments

It's nice to be able to sincerely thank one's children. Here I owe my initial attention to this subject to my two teenagers, Taylor and Haley. I thank our friends and relatives in the Pacific Northwest, whose concerns and questions about MySpace alerted me to the need for such a book when we visited them in the summer of 2006. Thanks to my family, coworkers, and friends who gave encouragement, prayers, and their two-cents' worth on this topic—particularly to Bud and Dianna Pitts along with their kids and grandkids (Sheila and Josh), to Velma Dingeman along with her kids and grandkids, and to Sherrie Lorance, who worked as my research assistant on this project.

Thanks also goes to the parents and families who opened up about their concerns on the subject, particularly: Julie and Piper Adams, Ashley Chase and her father, Curt Fetter, my husband, Patrick, and the parents who cared enough to come out on a Wednesday night to discuss their teens and MySpace at First Presbyterian Church of Roseville, California. I am also grateful to the senior pastor there, Dr. Jim Barstow, for his excellent and timely sermon on interaction between the five living generations. It affirmed the need for those of us over thirty to actively commit ourselves to staying connected to those in the Mosaic Generation. Thanks also for the use of his laptop computer early on in the writing.

I am grateful for two very informative and helpful conferences I attended during the writing of this book, and for all the work that went into assembling the experts and interested parties I was able to interview. The first was the Internet Evangelism Coalition's annual conference in Chicago on September 1, 2006, which focused on Christians and MySpace. There I learned of the many Christian "alternative

7

MySpace" sites, met the founders of Body of Christ Online (*boc.org*) and *MyPraize.com*. I was also able to listen carefully to the debate on this topic by Christian leaders involved in using the internet for ministry and family purposes.

The second was the California Cyber-Safety Summit presented by Governor Arnold Schwarzenegger and the California Department of Consumer Affairs (conveniently assembled in Sacramento, near my home). My immense thanks go to all the excellent presenters, keynote speakers, workshop leaders, organizers, and exhibitors who assembled October 18, 2006, for this summit. I especially thank those who took time to talk with me, answer my questions, and share information used in this book. These include: Officer Jan Hoganson of the Sacramento Sherriff's Department; Monique Nelson and Katie Canton of Web Wise Kids; Mark Klass of KlassKids Foundation; Larry Magid and Anne Collier, who authored *MySpace Unraveled* (a more computer-focused guide for parents that you may find helpful as a follow-up to this book); Joanne McNabb, Chief of California Office of Privacy Protection; Parry Aftab, Esq., and her Teen Angels of *WiredSafety.org*; Nancy E. Willard M.S., J.D. executive director of the Center for Safe and Responsible Internet Use; Stephen Kline, Chief Safety Officer for *Xanga.com* and former cyber-crime prosecutor; and Simrin Mangat, Manager of Safety and Security at Fox Interactive Media (parent company of MySpace).

The team at Zondervan has long been one of my favorite and most highly respected publishers. The editorial team led by Sandra Vander Zicht did stellar work (which had to be done at light speed!) to get this book ready for the public while it is still needed. I am deeply grateful to the editors—especially to Lori Vanden Bosch, who did such a fine job on the content editing—and to the copy editors and designers, who worked together to bring this book to you in a style that fits your needs. Each one played a crucial part. Thanks also to the team in marketing and publicity, who worked to let you know this book is here for you, and to all who helped get it into your hands so that you can use it to keep your teen safe and enhance your family's use of social networking sites on the internet.

Introduction

Welcome, parents, to the world of MySpace! Perhaps your teen has recently gotten involved with MySpace, and you're curious about this new phenomenon and want to learn more about it. Good for you! This book will give you a quick, sweeping overview of the MySpace world: what it is, where it came from, and why it is so popular. Beyond that, it shows how MySpace allows teens to do all the things that teens have always done in the past, but are now using a fascinating new medium.

If you are honest, though, you would probably have to admit that you're as frightened as you are curious about MySpace. You've heard lots of rumors about MySpace abuse, and your first instinct is to ban MySpace outright. Hold on. This book will give you the perspective and the practical tools you need to make wise, informed decisions about MySpace use.

Ultimately, however, your main reason for reading this book is that you love your child and want to be a good parent as you steer her through the turbulent waters of the teen years. This book not only introduces you to MySpace and how to use it safely, it also takes the final step: helping *you* to tailor *your teen's* use of MySpace to his current maturity level.

Whether you are computer illiterate or already an avid surfer of the Web, this book is for you. But don't just read it. Work with it. Apply it. Talk with your teen about it. In doing so, you'll not only explore MySpace, but you'll get a glimpse into the most precious space of all: your teen's thoughts, talents, and heart.

Let the journey begin!

Part 1

The MySpace Revolution

What Is MySpace?

I recently spoke to a woman who works for a parenting organization where I have previously spoken. I hoped to speak about MySpace for moms and dads at their upcoming national convention. She's a leader in her field and also has a teenage son, so I assumed she knew what I was talking about. As I carried on about "MySpace this" and "MySpace that," it slowly dawned on me that she hadn't a clue as to what I was talking about. She had never heard of MySpace.

So instead of trying to explain MySpace and convince her of how pervasive it is, I asked her to put down the phone and ask her thirteen-year-old son who, among his friends, had a MySpace page. I heard her ask him, and I heard him rattle off a list of names.

If you're among those thinking or asking, "MySpace? What's that?" don't feel bad. You're not alone. I commend you for venturing to find out!

▷ MySpace: It's Like a Whole New Language

There must be a teen in your life who's interested in MySpace. Otherwise you probably wouldn't be reading this book. If you're anything like me and many parents or grandparents I've talked to, exploring this whole "MySpace thing" feels something like learning a new language.

My two teenage children, Taylor and Haley, helped me set up a MySpace page when I wanted to learn about it several months ago. That seemed easy enough when they did it. So I wanted to make a new MySpace page specifically for readers of this book. The only problem was that I wanted to do this while they were at school, and I'm an impatient person. So I decided to give it a try.

I did okay. I managed to make my own MySpace page. I thought it looked pretty good. There was a small problem. For some reason unknown to me, it came out in German. I don't speak German.

So maybe learning MySpace *is* a bit like learning a whole new language. I didn't give up though! When Taylor and Haley got home from school, they showed me how to make a new page in English. It wasn't difficult. Once they stopped laughing, it was pretty easy to translate it to a language I could understand.

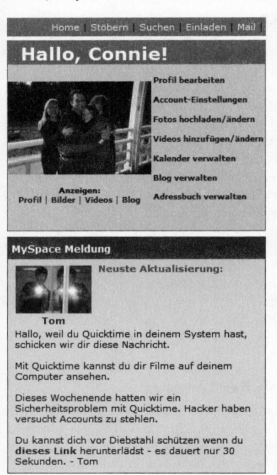

My children knew enough to help me take something that was foreign to me and make it understandable. The same principle can apply to what we're doing in this book. You will probably feel awkward; you'll make some mistakes; but you can do this with a little help (and maybe a little ribbing).

Fine—we don't know the technologies as well as our teens do. We may not even be comfortable using a computer. But we know enough. We know that we care about our teen. We know that these new ways of communicating are creating new dangers and they don't yet have the wisdom and life experience to navigate safely without some guidance. We know that most teens are using MySpace or some other social networking site. We also realize that we'd better figure out what this means for our teen's sake. That's why we're willing to deal with feeling like we're trying to learn a whole new language. Kudos to us! Good for our teens!

It's Not Really a Whole New Language

This exploration of MySpace is not really a whole new language. There are some new terms we need to become familiar with—which is why I've put a glossary at the back of the book. If you combine your knowledge of *your* teen, an adventurous spirit, a dose of patience, and whatever motivation you already have, that's enough to make a good start and learn the essentials about MySpace. We don't have to learn a whole new language. We only need someone to help us translate it.

For the purpose of making the "translation" easier and more fun, I recommend calling on a teen partner (preferably your own teen). Or you may want to do this with a group of supportive fellow learners with at least one knowledgeable guide. Perhaps your school PTA or local church will have enough interest to help you work though the rest of this book with other parents.

If you think your teen would *never* help you learn about MySpace, you may be right, but you may also be surprised. Teens hunger for parental attention and affirmation. Learning about MySpace presents an opportunity for both: there is the affirmation that you need her help because of her superior knowledge and experience in this area, and the attention that comes with that will be welcomed if it's not negative attention. Down the road you may be able to find some things on her MySpace profile that you can approve and applaud. It is worth looking into! If your teen is uncooperative, borrow help from a friend's teen or a group leader if you're in a group.

What Is Social Networking?

So what is MySpace? Simply put, MySpace and websites like it promote what's called *social networking*. Social networking may be a new phrase for you, since it is a relatively new term. Simply put, social networking is a way of using the computer and the internet so people can connect socially through computers. They can communicate back and forth with others who also have access to the internet. Technologies have advanced to the point where it is pretty easy for people to use a computer, not only to get information *from* the internet, but also to *contribute* content *to* the internet. Social networking sites have harnessed this power and made an easy way to connect with other people. People can send email, pass notes back and forth, and share music, ideas, photos, voice, videos, animations, and almost anything imaginable.

How to Describe MySpace

Have you heard the parable of the elephant and the blind men? It's told in many versions, but this one will serve our purposes.

The Parable of the Elephant and the Blind Men

Once upon a time, there lived six blind men in a village. One day the villagers told them, "Hey, there is an elephant in the village today."

They had no idea what an elephant was. They decided, "Even though we will not be able to see it, let us go and feel it anyway." All of them went to where the elephant was. Every one of them touched the elephant.

"Hey, the elephant is a pillar," said the first man who touched his leg.

"Oh, no! It is like a rope," said the second man who touched the tail.

"Oh, no! It is like a thick branch of a tree," said the third man, who touched the trunk of the elephant.

"It is like a big hand fan," said the fourth man, who touched the ear of the elephant.

"It is like a huge wall," said the fifth man, who touched the belly of the elephant.

"It is like a solid pipe," said the sixth man, who touched the tusk of the elephant.

They began to argue about the elephant, and every one of them insisted that he was right. It looked like they were getting agitated. A wise man was passing by and he saw this. He stopped and asked them, "What is the matter?"

They said, "We cannot agree on what the elephant is like." Each one of them told what he thought the elephant was like.

The wise man calmly explained to them, "All of you are right. The reason every one of you is telling it differently is because each one of you has touched a different part of the elephant. So actually the elephant has all those features you all said."

"Oh!" everyone said. There was no more fight. They felt happy that they were all right.[1]

Which Perspective Is Right?

Discussions about MySpace can become heated for the same reason battles broke out among the blind men arguing over the elephant. One person will declare it's nothing more than a pedophile's playground (and imply that any parent allowing their kids on MySpace is either ignorant or negligent, or simply doesn't care about their teen's safety).

Another person will say, "It's full of pornography and sexually suggestive photos. The majority of the photos on MySpace are *very* provocative."

Still another will state emphatically, "No! MySpace is an aspiring musician's best way to market his music."

A fourth person will say, "What are you talking about? It's a great way for a church group to discuss the Bible study for that week, ask questions, and compare notes."

Another will say, "Don't you know? It's the source of cyber-bullying, a new way to torment the rejects from school with rumors and ridicule."

Again, from someone else, "Oh, it's just a new way for politicians and advertisers to bombard us with messages we don't care to hear."

Still another will say, "It's a wonderful way to stay connected to your teens and hear what's going on in their hearts and minds, while training them in life skills."

You get the drift, and you could keep the conversation going with what you've heard about MySpace from the other parents you've talked to about it. And you have it on good authority, because each one is speaking from experience. When it comes to MySpace, we are pretty much in the dark about this new technological "animal." Whatever experience or knowledge we have with social networking is limited to some form of personal exploration, hearsay, limited personal experience, or alarming media reports. None of these grasps the whole.

How MySpace Is Like Xerox and Kleenex

Years back, if I was going to copy something on a copy machine, I said I was going to "Xerox" it. If I needed a tissue, I might ask someone to hand me a "Kleenex" regardless of what that brand of tissue might have been. These brand names became interchangeable with the generic description of the entire category because they were the first, or best, or most popular. That's sort of how it is with MySpace; if you have heard of social networking at all, you've probably heard of MySpace. It became by far the most popular social networking site and therefore garnered media attention.

There are currently hundreds of other social networking sites that have basically the same functions and serve similar purposes, with minor variations. It's anticipated that soon there will be thousands. Some of the most popular now include Xanga, Facebook, and Friendster. There are also a growing number of Christian MySpace alternatives, which I will discuss in the chapter "MySpace and Families of Faith."

Since MySpace is the front-runner and the others tend to have similar functions and formats, I have chosen to use MySpace as the basic template for exploring social networking. Even if your teen prefers a different social networking site, what you learn here about MySpace will apply to decisions about other sites as well. From this point on, I'm going to stop saying "MySpace and other social networking sites"; just know that what you learn here will generally apply across the board. Once you learn to navigate the basics of MySpace, you will be able to do the same on other social networking sites.

▷ Ask Your Teen

If you are coming to MySpace out of concern for your teen's well-being, much of what you need to know about MySpace falls under the category of what MySpace is to *your teen*. So at a basic level you can go a long way toward learning much of what you need to know about MySpace by asking your teen and listening intently. Throughout this book, therefore, I will be prompting you to talk with your teen with sections called "Ask Your Teen." Asking your teen won't work in all situations, but it's worth a try. Ask. Ask in a casual, nonthreatening way. Listen carefully; ask follow-up questions as they occur to you.

So let's try it. For your first question, ask something like, "Hey, would tell me what you know about MySpace? I'm curious. What *is* MySpace?" Don't grab your paper and pen just yet, but when the conversation is over, pick up your book and jot down a summary of what your teen tells you here:

Don't stop here. As occasions arise, ask people you know if they know what MySpace is. You will most likely prove to yourself that MySpace is *whatever* it is to each person, depending on what they have heard, how they use it, or what their experience has been. Do not argue with anyone; you're doing research. You are collecting an assortment of all the different parts and possibilities that make up this strange new "animal" that you are examining for the good of your teen.

Put notes on what people tell you MySpace *is to them* here:

_____

_____

_____

_____

_____

_____

Keep collecting various perspectives as you proceed with this adventure into the realm of social networking and MySpace.

Next we'll look at the origins of MySpace and how its advent has dramatically changed our world.

2

The World Has Changed

While visiting a family we know from church, I struck up a conversation with Curt, their fourteen-year-old son. I asked him, "Of all the kids in your eighth-grade class, how many would you guess have a MySpace page?"

Without missing a beat he replied, "Ninety-nine point nine percent, definitely! And I'm in the point-one percent." Wow! I guess that was his way of saying just about everybody's doing it. While that may be an exaggeration of the actual statistics for his school, he was fully convinced that *everybody* except him had a MySpace page.

As parents, we all know that the phrase "but everybody's doing it" begs for the classic parental reply: "I don't care what everybody else is doing. If Jimmy jumped off a cliff, would you?" But before we quip that we don't care what *everybody else* is doing, perhaps it would be good to understand the origins of MySpace and the social revolution MySpace is bringing to our teen's world.

The Birth of the Interactive Web

I graduated from college in 1980 as a communication major. My final paper dealt with a connected network of computers that would one day revolutionize the way people interact in our world. I was ahead of my time; the internet was still more than a decade away. In 1981 the National Science Foundation provided a grant to establish the Computer Science Network (CSNET) to provide networking services to all university computer scientists.[1] In 1986 the National Science Foundation connected all the supercomputers, thus creating the first "internet," known as NSFNET. Just six years later brought the World Wide Web, which led to 1993 being designated as the birth of the Mosaic Generation (those who grew up with the Web).

Use of the internet grew tremendously in 1994, with 100,000 web addresses or URL's registered. From 1993 to 1998 the internet became privatized and home computer sales skyrocketed. Today's teens, who were infants or toddlers in 1992, grew up right along with the internet. Is it any wonder they are comfortable using this as their primary means of interaction with others?

In the last three or four years, the way the internet affects our teens has changed dramatically again, primarily because of changes in how our teens use the internet. Up to 2002 or thereabouts, the internet was a provider of information (hopefully used for homework and reports, right?). But with the advent of what techies call Web 2.0 (the second level of use for the World Wide Web), users were able to easily *contribute* their own content. It became as easy as child's play for anyone to post things such as words, pictures, music, video, animations, and films on the internet and to invite others to view them and respond to them. The internet has become truly interactive to our teens, and they are eager to make the most of the new possibilities.

Thomas Friedman in his best-selling book *The World Is Flat* identified this trend away from passive consumption of media (TV, movie, and sports watching) to an active, participatory use of media (computer games, social networking, blogs, chat rooms, etc.). This generation doesn't just want to sit back and watch. They want to be involved, take part, contribute something.[2] Sites like MySpace are tapping into that desire and are changing our world in the process.

This major shift in the way the internet is used brought tremendous possibilities that the younger generation has responded to in unprecedented numbers. To them it was a wonderful, amazing, truly cool set of possibilities they simply could not resist exploring. Indeed, I will share with you and encourage you to explore some of these positive possibilities; it will help you understand what your teen is trying to tell you.

Simultaneous to this shift to Web 2.0, social networking took off. The first popular social networking sites were Facebook (which focused on connecting college students), Xanga (which focused on blogs and writing), and Friendster (which began as a dating site).

▷ The Origins of MySpace

MySpace began in 2003 with Tom Anderson (who is the first "friend" of every MySpace member) and Chris DeWolfe, who were part of the laid-back music scene of Santa Monica, California. They decided to create a way for LA-area musicians and bands to promote their music and upcoming gigs, connect with fans, and share their music online. MySpace allowed individual users to create—easily and for free—a page on the web with a personal profile, where bands could put up to four of their songs for anyone in the world to hear (and tell their friends about) and where users could communicate with each other and assemble a network of friends. The site quickly became popular with teens and twenty-somethings, and within two years it leaped from a popular music site to a mega-phenomenon.

By March 2004 MySpace had "accumulated 67 million members since its launch" and was "growing by an average of 250,000 new members daily," said Dani Dudeck, a MySpace spokeswoman.[3] By the summer of 2006 MySpace boasted 100,000,000—that's one hundred *million*—MySpace pages.

In 2006, media mogul Rupert Murdoch, famous for building one of the largest media empires in the world, with interests in TV, pay TV, films, newspapers, publishing, and the internet, bought MySpace for $580 million. Murdoch was asked by a Reuters reporter, "What surprised you most about the MySpace experience?"

His answer? "The speed at which it has grown ... And it just grows faster and faster every week ... MySpace demonstrated what we felt but now really drives it into us that the world has really changed—that the average person who is computer proficient is self-empowered in their lives in a way they never have [been] before."[4]

▷ A New Way of Thinking

Have you looked at a MySpace page or websites in general and found the jumble of images and content jarring? You're not alone. Those of us who did not grow up with the internet have brains conditioned from our childhood to see the things we read arranged in an orderly fashion. We learned most of our early knowledge from the pages of books— pages that followed one after another with type in line upon orderly line, going from left to right.

Our teens grew up as part of what's been called the Millennial Generation, or Generation X, also known as the Mosaics. The term *Mosaics* is most helpful for us in understanding why we are uncomfortable with the visual display of MySpace and they are not.

Their generation grew up learning as much from computer screens and websites as they learned from books. Their brains learned to accept information that was laid out digitally. They don't expect information to be laid out line upon line. They are used to it being jumbled together, chunks of meaning in haphazard array from which they can choose, like tiles in a mosaic. They regularly check out one thing, click to a new page, then go back to check out another, or take a link to an entirely new site filled with—what appears to us to be—a jumble of new possibilities. So don't be surprised if you feel ill at ease when you first start checking out MySpace pages. It may never be your preferred form of communication, but we do a lot of things that stretch us for our kids' sake. Press past your generational discomfort with the form and it will pay off in a better understanding of your teen and your teen's world.

▷ Think Big, Really Big

When we think of the magnitude of the MySpace revolution, we need to think big. The cultural changes and possibilities coming about because of the social networking revolution are monumental. Think in terms like going from getting around by horse and buggy on rutted dirt roads to zooming along at seventy miles per hour on paved highways in modern cars. We have no way to accurately gauge the change that is taking place right now, but some experts think it may be in that league.

As with all previous technological advances, there is no going back to life as it was. Each new advancement brings with it new dangers and requires new skills to manage the greater power at our command. Since MySpace and social networking sites are not going away, our teens will benefit from our help in learning to manage this new technology for their good.

Many of the parents I speak with about MySpace wonder how this got to be such a cultural phenomenon without them knowing this was

happening. Don't feel bad; this happened fast! Probably the only reason it came to our attention was publicity over the dangers and new
possibilities it opened up for predators. MySpace is our wake-up call
to see that our teen's world has really changed and is changing *fast*. So
we must move quickly to keep pace, and we can. As my son says, "This
isn't rocket surgery." It's new, but it doesn't have to be daunting.

MySpace is not just a fad. While users may move around from
MySpace to other social networking sites, they have come to see social
networking on some site as part of their lives. The way this generation
relates and communicates through the new media of social networking
sites and the internet marks a shift in the way our teens' generation
thinks, interacts, and relates to their world. If we keep pace, we can
help make that a positive change for the teens we love.

In my research, I have encountered two types of parents and their
responses to this new cultural phenomenon:

- parents who try to understand and stay connected to their teen
  in the process
- parents who resist, ignore, or reject this monumental change
  (and get left behind as their teen adapts to his or her rapidly
  changing world without their help)

If MySpace and sites like it are indicators of a societal shift that is
as monumental as the invention of the car was for life in the Western
world, isn't it far better for teens to navigate these dramatic changes
with the help of a concerned parent? If we deprive them of such help,
they will be left to deal with these issues guided by the barrage of advice from friends who are experiencing this revolution with them.

I heartily recommend that you be the first kind of parent: try to
understand. Once you do understand, you may still decide against
MySpace use for a particular teen at a particular time of life. However,
by becoming fully informed about MySpace, you will be better able
to make such decisions with confidence. You will also be equipped
to offer your teen guidance about how to adapt to this revolutionary
change in a safe and positive way. I commend you for doing so!

▷ Ask Your Teen

1. What percentage of your classmates would you guess have a
   page on MySpace or a similar social networking site?

   _____

   _____

   _____

   _____

2. How would you say MySpace and sites like it have changed the
   way your friends and classmates communicate with each other?

   _____

   _____

   _____

   _____

   _____

"Okay," you may be saying. "I understand the basics of what MySpace
is and how popular it is. But what's the big deal? Why do teens seem to
like it so much?" That's the topic of our next chapter.

3

Why Teens Love MySpace

What has the power to make young men weep?

If you guessed being banned from MySpace, you're right. I recently attended a conference sponsored by the Internet Evangelism Coalition. One of the panel discussions included four Christian leaders involved in internet ministries who were also parents of teens. The discussion addressed the dangers of MySpace.

Early on, one of the men mentioned that by the time he caught up with the MySpace scene, he browsed around enough to decide that he did not want his sixteen-year-old son participating. He told his son he would have to delete his profile and close his MySpace account. The man confessed to being taken by surprise when his son began to weep.

One after another, three of the four panelists revealed that the same thing had happened with their teenage son or daughter. Each parent declared that the MySpace profile would have to be deleted and the account shut down; each one of the teens came to tears. The fourth allowed his son to participate on MySpace under his supervision.

Apparently, there is something about MySpace that has the power to bring teens to tears—even young men who aren't prone to such displays of emotion. This issue has the potential to be *hugely* important to many of our teens.

▷ How Teens Use MySpace to Do What Teens Have Always Done

There's no blanket explanation that covers every individual teen, but there are reasons that generally explain why teens typically love

MySpace (although I have met the occasional teen who *hates* MySpace and declares loudly she will never have a page).

King Solomon, the wisest of the wise, declared that there is nothing new under the sun — including MySpace. While the technology is new to us, what teens are using social networking *to do* is not new. Basically, teens are able to do on MySpace all those things that teens *need* to do as they pass through the developmental phase of adolescence. The technology removes some of the hesitations, creates a greater sense of anonymity (which is one of the reason parents worry and something we need to discuss with our teens), multiplies their reach, empowers them, and feeds their curiosity. Yes, they may now have immediate access to almost anything or anyone who attracts their attention, but essentially teens still want what teens have always wanted.

Here is a brief rundown of the general needs in a teen's life that MySpace fulfills in various ways. Teens need to:

- communicate with friends and peers
- express themselves
- discover who they truly are (by trying on various personas, hairstyles, styles of dress, etc.)
- see what other people are like
- explore the voice of their generation by listening to music
- view artistic expressions (photography, paintings, and murals)
- hear, see, or read stories (books, TV, movies, plays)
- flirt with each other

More than almost anything they want to:

- make and keep friends
- be included
- belong to a group

Let's look at some of these more closely. Later, in Part 3 ("How Teens Use MySpace"), I will show you more specifically how MySpace functions in each of these areas.

Connecting and Communicating with Friends and Peers

Teens need to connect with their friends and peers. They need to share the ups and downs of their personal lives, get help with school projects, express their concerns to someone who cares, and stay close to their friends. They need to talk, to be heard. They need to know they belong to a social group.

When we were teens, we did this primarily on the telephone. But for many teens, MySpace is a better option. It allows a myriad of ways to connect with friends and peers. Sometimes it provides a safer social option than calling on the phone. It multiplies their reach by allowing them to communicate with many friends at once. It allows them to leave their imprint so others (who have visited the same MySpace page) can see what they communicated.

Self-Expression

Every human being is born with a need to express himself or herself. It can be argued that teens need to express themselves more than people at other times of life because they are discovering who they are, what they believe, what their talents are, and who cares about them. These are important developmental tasks. As teens express themselves on MySpace, they can get feedback in comments and kudos. It gives them a way to determine for themselves what they have that is of unique value to share with the world.

One of my favorite books says something along these lines. Consider this quote in terms of your teen and his or her need for self-expression (particularly on MySpace). It comes from the book written in 1938: *If You Want to Write*, by Brenda Ueland; it is still on my shelf today for good reason. What she says here will help you understand the appeal of MySpace for teens.

Everybody is talented, original, and has something important to say.[1]

Everybody is talented because everybody who is human has something to express. Try *not* expressing anything for twenty-four hours and see what happens. You will nearly burst. You will want to write a long letter or draw a picture or sing, or make a dress or a garden. Religious men used to go into the wilderness and impose silence on themselves, but it was so that they would talk to God and nobody else. But they expressed something: that is to say they had thoughts welling up in them and the thoughts went out to someone, whether silently or aloud. Writing or painting is putting these thoughts on paper. Music is singing them. That is all there is to it.[2]

Enter MySpace and social networking. Now teens can express themselves in numerous ways and get immediate feedback to let them know if anyone is listening, or looking, or caring. Given their busy lives, working parents, disconnected extended families, and many other cultural facts of life, teens in this generation sometimes lack the kind of attention they crave and need. The opportunity to express oneself in various ways and to find someone out there who cares and pays attention is very gratifying.

Going Places and Doing Things

One of the upsides to being a teen is a greater freedom to go places and do things without being under the constant supervision of parents. Teens begin to venture out in social activities. They get invited to parties, get-togethers, and school events; and they need to know when everybody from their group is going to be at the skating rink.

"What's happening?" is more than just a popular phrase; it's something teens need to know. Social networking makes this easier. Beyond just letting friends and family know of their events, teens like to know what their options are. Using the Events feature on MySpace, they can find out if there are any events in a particular category in their area in the near future.

Growing Independence

The teenage years are all about growing in independence (and interdependence with a circle larger than one's immediate family). The ability to explore various media — music, movies, film, TV, comedy, and so on — gives teens a chance to explore their personal preferences as they grow more independent.

Social networking offers teens several ways in which to consider various beliefs, investigate groups, listen in on forums, and work out their developing sense of independent thought. They can also meet new people and get involved in any aspect of life that catches their interest by meeting others who share that interest. This can be very positive; for example, a mathematically gifted teen whose family does not share this interest might find like-minded friends online who are similarly gifted, know all about robotics, and can share that knowledge, even if they don't live in the same geographical location. In this way the teen is able to individuate and develop a particular gifting.

This is also a danger zone, if teens venture into groups where people are not who they pretend to be, or if teens exert their independence in socially unacceptable, rebellious, or dangerous ways.

Flirting with Attraction/Emerging Sexuality

Teens are at that age when biology dictates that they will become more aware of and attracted to the opposite sex or will struggle with their gender identity. They will flirt; boys will enjoy looking at attractive girls and girls looking at that cute boy. All teens enjoy others finding them attractive enough to flirt with. Teens have always practiced boy-girl relationships.

MySpace makes it much easier for teens to get to "know" or check out someone they may find attractive but don't know well. They can check out a profile and see if there is some common interest that might give them something to talk about. They can communicate in a more casual way than making a phone call or asking someone out. They can use MySpace to eliminate potential romantic interests, as well as qualify them, without being seen. What's not to like about that if you're a teen?

Finding One's Place in the Larger World

Part of growing up is venturing out into the world. When you have social networking and the internet, you can venture out from home without leaving the safety of home. You can meet people and "make friends" in places around the world. You can find someone who loves the same books you do and supports the same social causes you believe in. With MySpace a teen can see what is happening in the world and figure out how to make a difference. That's attractive to idealistic teens.

Generally speaking, parents can probably accept that there are valid reasons teens love MySpace. These reasons explain why it has grown so quickly among the younger set. As we conclude this chapter, think about your teen. Take a few moments to write out what you think your teen would most enjoy about MySpace within the general categories I covered. Later in the book you will specifically ask your teen what aspects of MySpace most appeal to her. When you do that exercise ("Ask Your Teen: How would you use MySpace? How much does this feature of MySpace matter to you?" on page 146), you can compare the answers she gives you there to the answers you've written below. You'll get a glimpse into how well you know your teen.

▷ Ask Yourself

1. In the area of communicating with friends and peers, what do you think your teen would enjoy about what MySpace lets them do?

   _____

   _____

2. In the area of self-expression, what do you think your teen would enjoy about what MySpace lets them do?

   _____

   _____

3. In the area of going places and doing things, what do you think your teen would enjoy about what MySpace lets them do?

   _____

   _____

4. In the area of growing independence, what do you think your teen would enjoy about what MySpace lets them do?

   _____

   _____

5. In the area of flirting and romantic or sexual attraction, what do you think your teen would enjoy about what MySpace lets them do?

   _____

   _____

6. In the area of finding one's place in the larger world, what do you think your teen would enjoy about what MySpace lets them do?

_____

_____

Before we take a look at the MySpace website itself, let's pause to talk about safety on MySpace, since that is the topic parents are most concerned about.

4

Who's in Charge
of Safety on MySpace?

The audience in the Sacramento Convention Center, October 18, 2006, was a who's who of the most powerful and influential leaders in the area of internet safety, gathered for the first Cyber-Safety Summit. There were senators, a former secretary of the treasury, leaders from Microsoft, people from MySpace, and the chief security officer from Xanga. There were district attorneys, the Sheriffs Association, the state Parent Teacher Association, the School Board Association, representatives from leading internet safety organizations like Web Wise Kids, the National Center of Missing and Exploited Children, WiredSafety.com, NetSmartz, and the media. Representatives from government, public interests, business, education, law enforcement, and parents filled the large assembly hall at the convention center.

▷ Who Bears the Most Responsibility?

At the Cyber Safety Summit we were all given a handheld device so that the audience could be polled immediately in response to what we were hearing. Given that this was a specialized gathering of cyber-safety experts, I was very interested in learning our combined estimation of the current situation. One of the questions that impacted me most directly, since I was there as a concerned parent of teens, was this one: "Who should bear the most responsibility for safety of underage users (teens or kids) on the internet? Parents? Industry/Business? Schools? Peers?" Insofar as this event was sponsored by a state government agency, I was surprised government was not on the list. The answers from this audience?

92% believed parents should bear the most responsibility.

6% believed industry/business (that would include MySpace.com).
1% said schools.
1% said peers.

So these cyber-safety experts agreed that you and I *should* bear the most responsibility for our teen's internet safety. But among parents, I hear a lot of talk blaming MySpace. I suspect you do too.

Therefore, I was interested when Craig Hill of the National Center for Missing and Exploited Children was asked how well he thought the social networking sites were doing with regard to safety issues. He not only works for a child protection agency, he's a thirty-five-year police veteran and expert on online safety. Although he was asked about social networking in general, he answered, "MySpace and social networking are like anything else. The greatest danger is to users who don't know how to use it safely. I think all the bad PR MySpace has received is unfair. MySpace is blamed because it's the most popular. If you ask me who's going to make the most difference in kids' safety on social networking sites, it's not government. Not police. Not MySpace. It's the parents; they have to step up and take the lead."

▷ Predators versus Protectors

Sometimes we parents seem to be cowering in fear over these predators as though we have no power. Something deeply bothers me about this! Why should the predators use the power of online social networking to threaten or harm our teens without us fighting back? The power of the internet can work for our teen's protectors every bit as much as it works for the predators. However, that requires us to get involved. So I again commend you for working through this book. You can join the forces of the protectors who refuse to abdicate to the predators and back away to simply wring your hands.

I was pleased and encouraged when I read the story of a mother of a teenage girl who was beaten by a group of classmates at her high school. This protective mom didn't allow her daughter to have a MySpace page, but she was aware enough to use MySpace on her daughter's behalf. At the prompting of a friend of her daughter, she realized that the girls who beat her up went to her school and probably had a MySpace page. With coaching from her daughter's friend, she searched through the MySpace profiles of students who identified themselves as attending that school. Her daughter and friend were able to identify one of the attackers from her photo on her profile. They went to her profile page—which was public—and checked her "friends" list. There were the smiling faces of the other three attackers. With this information, she alerted the police and school administrators, and the attackers were caught and charged with assault. Way to go, Mom!

That's the approach we need to take. We need to harness the power of this new technology to fight back against the predators and attackers who want to harm our teens. Yes, the predators have a head start, but we can catch up. We can make a difference by becoming aware and actively protective in the MySpace neighborhood.

Here's how:

- We can report abuse to MySpace (more on how to do that later).
- We can report inappropriate content to MySpace.
- We can report to MySpace underage users or older users who are misrepresenting themselves as younger in order to be able to peruse younger teens' profiles.
- We can use MySpace as the mom in the above story did to monitor the safety of our teens in the real world, and if necessary contact local authorities to alert them of harm that has been done or harm that someone may be planning.

Another alert parent noticed that a group of teens seemed to be planning a "Columbine-style" attack at their high school. The police were notified. They too used MySpace to monitor communication between the would-be attackers and discover their plans. When they searched the homes of those involved, they found numerous weapons that were intended to inflict untold death and destruction. But they were stopped by an alert adult looking out for the welfare of high school students in another part of the country using MySpace.

See, we can outwit the would-be evildoers. Protectors can overcome the ploys and plans of the predators by making the technology work for us and for the good of our teens. That does require us to invest ourselves in learning how to navigate the social networking world and spend some time doing so. You've already begun.

I refuse to cower before the predators. I want to overcome evil with good! And I intend to do so. This book is a step in that direction. No one of us can turn the tide alone, but we are not alone. Besides, even on our own, each one of us can protect our teens by being knowledge-able and proactive regarding their social networking activities. If every parent concerned about MySpace would *do something*, we could put the predators on the run or behind bars. That does my heart good! And it would do our teens good too!

▷ MySpace Safety Efforts to Keep Teens Safe

One of the speakers at the Cyber-Safety Summit was Mark Klass, who became a child-safety advocate after his twelve-year-old daughter, Polly Klass, was abducted from her home in 1993 and murdered. Given that Mark Klass had lost his daughter to a sexual predator, and given (as he told us) that police estimate there are approximately fifty thousand predators online at any given moment, it surprised me to hear him talking so favorably about MySpace safety efforts. From the podium, he said, "MySpace is not the embodiment of evil. They have five human filters for every image. They have taken responsibility as a social net-work for their content."

Here Mr. Klass was referring to the levels of screening in place to review images that are flagged as potentially inappropriate. All im-ages posted on MySpace are reviewed, although not before appearing on a user's page. Those that are reported as inappropriate get greater scrutiny. If they violate the terms of use, they are deleted by MySpace, along with the user's profile. This is certainly not the impression I had gotten from the news media.

Since I have previously worked as a researcher looking for inaccuracy and bias in the news media, I wasn't too surprised that the sensational stories of predators on MySpace had been taken out of context. So I did a little research of my own to give the alarming stories of sexual predators on MySpace some context.

MySpace works with the National Center for Missing and Exploited Children and law enforcement agencies. Anytime they find content on MySpace that could be a violation of the law, they report it to the NCMEC cyber-tip line. They also freeze the pages, deny access to the user, check the Friends pages, and turn it over to law enforcement. How often do they do this? About twelve times a month. Hmmm ... twelve times a month out of over 100,000,000 MySpace pages. That gives it some context. Illegal content is far less prevalent than the media makes it appear to be. In addition, MySpace deletes the profiles of underage users who have lied to get a MySpace page approximately 20,000 times per week.

So MySpace is trying to make social networking safe for our teens. Fox Interactive Media (MySpace's parent company, "FIM") recently hired Hemanshu Nigam as chief security officer. Nigam has sixteen years of safety and security experience as a former federal and state prosecutor and is also experienced in the movie and software industries. He formerly led child-safe computing at the Microsoft Corporation. Prior to that, he was a trial attorney for the United States Department of Justice, Criminal Division, specializing in child pornography, child predator, and child online protection issues.

The *Wall Street Journal* interviewed Hemanshu Nigam on July 24, 2006. He said, "Our top priority right now is to find or build the right set of technologies that will make the internet and MySpace safer for teens." But, he added, "whatever technical solutions we implement can only be successful if they're coupled with a mom or a dad teaching their teens how to be safe online." So MySpace is doing their part, but they need each of us to do our part as well.

I don't have the authority, but if I did, I would designate each parent of a teen who uses a computer as the chief security officer of their own family. At this moment, who is the chief security officer for your teen? We don't have the extensive background that Mr. Nigam has, but we have an advantage; we're *there* with our teen and we have love. That goes a long way toward keeping them safe.

▷ The Most Important Person in the Room

The Cyber-Safety Summit in Sacramento included a surprise guest: former Mr. Universe, mega-movie star, and governor of California, Arnold Schwarzenegger. I was already impressed by the assembly, but I must admit being even more impressed with Governor Schwarzenegger. He looks good for fifty-nine, solid, certainly powerful physically as well as politically. He greeted the audience and expressed his gratitude, saying, "Every organization that is here today and every individual, I want to say thank you very much for participating here, because all of your work is extremely important to keep our kids safe."

It was hard to separate out the "Arnold" I had seen in *The Termina-tor* and other films from the public servant, especially when he came to the end of his speech. Please try to imagine him saying these words in his classic Arnold accent, but looking every bit as determined as the "Governator" as he did in any movie role. He looked the audience in the eye and said, "And let's be vigilant, because our children deserve nothing less."

Are you imagining this in *his* voice? That really makes a difference. He went on, "And also, let's send a clear message here to all the cyber predators out there ... to all the cowards who want to make victims out of our children ... that we are coming after you ... that we will find you ... and that we will punish you."

Applause broke out as Governor Schwarzenegger thanked us again. At that moment—early in the day—I would have conceded that he was probably the most powerful person in the room. After all, he had the leadership role and power that had brought the rest of us there for the Cyber-Safety Summit, not to mention his Kennedy connections, movie-star status, physical strength, and political clout.

However, as I listened to speaker after speaker, expert after expert, they all agreed that he was *not* the most powerful person in the room. According to them, *I* was; that is, any *involved parent* has the most power and influence to keep their kids and teens safe online. Among the best and brightest who have devoted themselves to internet safety, every one of them agreed on that point. Wow! That was both sobering and exciting.

If that is indeed the case—and it made sense the way each one ex-plained it—you and I hold the power to make using MySpace or any social networking site a positive and protected experience for the teens we love. That's good news. It's especially promising given that you have picked up this book. Not only do you have the potential power—power no one else can wield if you neglect it—you also have been motivated to take action. Good for you, and better for your teens.

▷ What's My Motivation?

Let's look at your motivation, because it is important and relevant to whether you will carry out using your power for the good of your teen in this arena. I'd guess that a high percentage of parents who have picked up this book are doing so primarily because of fear. We have all heard reports of teens being lured into dangerous situations by sexual predators. We've read news stories of teens misusing their MySpace pages, making threats, bragging about illegal activities, harassing their peers, and slandering teachers and school administrators.

We've probably seen or at least heard about the *Dateline* series "To Catch a Predator," where adult men who think they're communicating online with young teen girls or boys make arrangements to meet for sex, then are apprehended by law enforcement after being captured and confronted on camera. It's enough to raise the hair on the back of the neck of any protective mom or dad, especially when several of the "predators" don't look like the monsters we expect. Some of them are disclosed to be pastors, rabbis, church youth ministry volunteers, and otherwise "nice guys." There are also sensational teasers for TV news reports that get us to stay up a bit later to watch the broadcast if there's a story related to teens and internet predators. It's no wonder we're scared.

Fear Motivation

The stories that scare us boost ratings and increase circulation for media outlets. Fear is a strong motivator to get us to watch and to read, which brings us back to why you picked up this book. We have good reason to be afraid of the emerging dangers to our teens.

The world has changed, significantly. This point was stressed repeatedly by numerous speakers at the California Cyber-Safety Summit. Fifteen years ago—maybe while we were planning the nursery for that baby who has now become a young man or young woman—law enforcement had pretty much contained child sexual predators and distributors of child pornography. Laws to prosecute them were set and effective. All we had to do was look out for predators in real life, at the park or mall or bus stop.

But the internet changed everything, opening up a way for sexual predators to share pornography online, to encourage each other in their perversion, and to prowl for victims without leaving home—while invading ours. That raises legitimate fears.

With this new technology and easy access to the World Wide Web, the doors swung wide open for sexual predators, criminals, scammers, and all manner of unsavory characters to have access to the kids and teens we love. Meanwhile, kids and teens were projecting themselves into cyberspace freely without most adults realizing that anything had changed. So they were basically unsupervised, and the online predators—usually more computer-savvy than most parents—recognized their window of opportunity and were busy browsing. That's scary, but let's not stop at the point of our fears. Remember, I have it on good authority that *you* are the most powerful person in the room.

Somewhere along the line you heard about it, but what we parents heard was not only the buzz of something cool according to our kids and teens. Indeed, they may have been keeping it quiet, either not realizing the monumental nature of the change nor the alarming dangers they had incurred without noticing. By the time we heard about MySpace, we were hearing the wail of media alarms, magnifying the danger and causing us to be concerned for our teen's online safety, especially on sites like MySpace. This brings us back to our fear motivation.

There's nothing like a jolt of fear to get the adrenaline pumping, heart racing, and body primed for fight or flight. In this case, we want our teens to take flight from MySpace and avoid the fights that come when they resist. Fear motivation works great to get us moving, but if we live in a continued state of fear, tension, and high anxiety, we get worn down. So while fear can be a helpful starter in times of danger, we need a way to move on from fear to action that can resolve the tension. I'm going to show you how to do that as we proceed.

Think about your fear; does it include the fear that you may not be making the right decision about MySpace for your teen? If you've said no to MySpace for your teen, you may fear that you are being overprotective and may be harming your relationship with your teen as well as your teen's relationships with friends. If you say yes, you may fear that you are putting your teen at risk and not being a good parent by protecting them from all the dangers you've heard about. You may also fear that your teen, knowing more than you do about MySpace, can get around any prohibitions you set at home.

You are probably right if you have that fear. Teens can access MySpace or any of the other hundreds—soon to be thousands—of social networking sites from any desktop computer, laptop computer, wireless hand-held devices, and many cell phones. No wonder we're in a state of high anxiety.

If your anxiety level is soaring by now, please hold on. The way to reduce your anxiety is to gain clarity about whatever is causing the fear, make wise choices, do the best you can to avert danger, and as a result live a safer and happier life.

Reward Motivation

If your fear motivation gets you started, reward motivation can help keep you moving. Perhaps the only reward you can think of now is to resolve the unrelenting conflict with your teen over social networking. That's a good motivation. But the rewards available to you are far greater than you probably imagine. If you've already done some exploring on MySpace, you've probably discovered the many positive rewards of social networking.

Recently, for example, the percentage of MySpace users has shifted so that 78 percent are over eighteen. This may be partly because parents, checking out MySpace to quell their fears, are discovering the rewards of social networking for themselves. So don't discount reward motivation; going on MySpace can be more fun and more rewarding than you probably expect. However, reward motivation alone is not enough to carry you all the way through either. There's always the old stand-by—guilt.

Guilt Motivation

Several of the parents I talked with about MySpace expressed a lingering sense of guilty confusion. If Mom or Dad is uncertain about social networking while being asked by their teen to allow them to participate, most likely you will feel guilty no matter what you say. If you allow it, you may feel a vague guilt that perhaps you are putting your teen at risk; if you disallow it, you may feel guilty about disappointing your teen or keeping him or her from something they want. Residual guilt, like residual fear or anxiety, isn't good for anyone. Vague guilt comes along with uncertainty and confusion.

Many people are compelled by guilt motivation, which can really be a drag if it is carried on too long without resolution. But a well-working conscience and true guilt are valuable guides for life. True guilt points out wrongdoing and causes us enough pain to move us to address that which is wrong and hopefully turn around to do what is right.

So we have good news here too. Reading this book will help you gain clarity about what MySpace is and how your teen is using it, as well as about the relevant dangers that need to be countered. Now we can look at what safety precautions need to be taken by your teen to stay safe. This clarity will reduce your uncertainty and eliminate confusion over this matter. That will get rid of your guilt. If you are doing something wrong with regard to your teen's safety, you will discover that and learn what to do to correct it (and it will be simple enough for you to do).

According to cyber-safety experts, what most parents are guilty of related to social networking include: neglecting to learn about it (whatever social networking sites their teen uses or whatever their teen is doing online) or simply forbidding it (as if that solves the problems, which it does not). If you continue through this book, you will be guilty of neither. You may decide to forbid aspects of social networking for your teen at this time, or you may decide to forbid the use of certain sites in preference of another you deem more suitable, but you will make these as informed choices rather than ignorant, frightened choices. Therefore, your guilt motivation can be traded in for the best motivation of all—perhaps, the secret to our enormous power—the motivation of love.

The Best Motivation of All: Love

The great literature and art of all time extols love as the most powerful of motivators, perhaps the most powerful force on earth. The Bible goes so far as to declare, "Love never fails" (1 Corinthians 13:8). How's that for boosting your confidence? You may not know anything about MySpace or the internet or social networking, but you *know* that you *love* your teen. My task is to direct that love motivation into action that will keep you moving past the obstacles that may cause you to avoid becoming informed enough about social networking to make sure your teen is as safe as can be.

You truly do have the upper hand and the potential power to thwart the ploys of the predators in order to protect your teen. There are far too many parents—no doubt, loving parents—who get hung up on their hesitations and fail to venture into this new area of concern. Their teens, sadly, are left at greater risk because—experts agree—an involved parent is the greatest hindrance of any kind to an online predator.

If you follow through with the reading, discussions, and activities in this book, you can make sure that your teen will not be an appealing target for predators. You will be equipped to help your teen be able to interact in positive and protected ways on MySpace or any other social networking site, while also gaining life skills that will keep him or her safer in face-to-face relationships as well. Your love is the best motivation, with power enough to get you past the common obstacles that typically get in the way of many well-meaning parents.

▷ Common Obstacles to Overcome

Don't get stopped by the common obstacles that tend to get in our way when we approach MySpace and social networking. I find that taking the obstacles one by one reduces them to manageable proportions so we can get past any that might impede us. As I took on this project—first as a personal project, then to help other parents—I had to get past these obstacles myself. Because I know how you feel, I have taken care to do all I can to give you a boost to help you scale each of these. See which of these obstacles cause you to hesitate, then let the power of your love and all the other motivators you have working for you propel you to overcome them.

Obstacle #1: It's Overwhelming!

There is so much information out there, and so much media attention being paid to MySpace, social networking, and internet safety, that it can seem overwhelming. I know; I've read hundreds of articles and books, attended conferences, interviewed experts, watched everything I can find on TV, and searched the internet for everything about MySpace and social networking. That is what led me to decide against sharing all of that with you, or even to try to summarize it all. I have only given you what I think will help you make sure your teen is safe. So don't let yourself be overwhelmed. Keep your focus on the essentials.

Obstacle #2: Discomfort Using the Computer or Ignorance of Computer Terminology

This can be a big obstacle, especially if you are trying to get information *about* social networking and safety precautions but you are not comfortable accessing information online. However, I'll show you how to monitor your teen's social networking without having to operate a computer yourself. You may want to enlist the help of a willing mentor (perhaps even your teen), but you won't *have* to be computer literate to keep your child safe on MySpace.

Obstacle #3: I'm Too Busy!

We're all busy, but we make time to do those things that (1) we deem a priority and (2) we feel we can accomplish. If this were a project to comprehend all aspects of internet safety or even all aspects of MySpace, its various uses, and its myriad dangers, we would all probably throw up our hands and deem ourselves too busy (which would lead us back to obstacle #1, being overwhelmed), and we would stop or put off beginning. But that's not the aim of this book. This book is designed to help you understand MySpace, analyze your teen's use of this website, and find ways to help *your* teen to stay safe on MySpace.

Chapter 16 contains a safety checklist for busy parents so you can have your teen take you through a spot inspection. Periodically, you will check on MySpace to make sure the safety precautions you require are maintained. You can tailor this spot inspection to your teen's level of maturity. That will save lots of time!

⏮ ⏭

Those are the big three hesitations most parents encounter: feeling overwhelmed, being computer illiterate, and feeling too busy. There are other concerns that may play some part in your hesitations: fear that you might discover something about your teen or your teen's friends that you don't really want to know, concern that you might become addicted to social networking yourself, perceived conflicts with your religious faith, and so on. You can fill in the blank. Seriously. I've given you the space here to identify what obstacles cause you to hesitate to learn enough about MySpace to keep your teens safe. Write them here:

_____

_____

_____

_____

Identifying an obstacle is the first step to overcoming it. Facing an important issue is the first step to taking care of it. You are already on your way. Even if you have some hesitations that give you pause, even ones you can't resolve fully now, does that really stop you from trying to learn and do as much as you can to keep your child safe? No.

Remember, even though there are hundreds of politicians, business leaders, cyber-safety experts, law enforcement officers, and community leaders generally interested in "public safety," you are the one in your teen's world who has the access, influence, and responsibility to keep your teen as safe as can be. You have the motivation. You have the love. *You are the most powerful person in the room!*

Now let's venture into the world of MySpace and see how it works. We'll begin to do that in the next chapter by taking a tour of the virtual MySpace visitor's center.

Part 2

Exploring MySpace: An Introduction to the Site

5

Welcome to the MySpace Visitor's Center

You may remember the Randy Newman song "I Love LA!" It was popular during the 1984 Los Angeles Olympics. One of my favorite memories of Los Angeles was when we were walking through Westwood (an LA neighborhood near UCLA) during festivities surrounding the Olympics. The seventeen-story side of the West Los Angeles Federal Building was used as a giant screen for a laser show highlighting the good life in Los Angeles, accompanied by the song "I Love LA!" being carried across the warm evening air. I had to sing along! "I love LA!"

I *do* love LA; I grew up there and I know the entire metropolitan Los Angeles area very well. I know it well enough to know that there are many neighborhoods I would never visit in broad daylight, much less take my teens there. I certainly would never let them go unescorted or with a group of their friends. I love LA, but I also know that the LA area has gang activity, murders, rapes, robberies, and all manner of crime (not to mention some less-than-friendly residents). All of that takes place in every other major metropolitan area where large populations of people come together.

Knowing all of that does not keep me or my teens from visiting the Los Angeles metro area. Dare we forget that this area is home to "The Happiest Place on Earth" (Disneyland) and many other fine attractions? It is precisely *because* I know this area well enough to recognize and avoid the danger zones that I am free to enjoy all the wonderful parts of the Los Angeles experience.

I can give great guided tours. I did that once with my daughter Casey and six other teenage girls who went with me to LA for a youth evangelism conference in 2000. Some of those girls' parents were leery of Los Angeles, having never lived there and having heard scary things

49

about it. However, because I knew my way around—while being aware of real dangers we might encounter—I was able to ease their anxieties and convince them that the girls would be fine.

We stayed at the classic Biltmore Hotel. I took them downtown to world-famous Olvera Street—home of the most delicious authentic Mexican food. We visited the La Brea Tar Pits and went to the Museum of Science and Industry. We drove down Wilshire Boulevard through Beverly Hills zip code 90210 (with a stroll down Rodeo Drive). We went past Century City, home of the Schubert Theatre, then drove past Westwood and UCLA, showing them cool bookstores, churches, and restaurants along the way. Finally we ended up at the Pacific Ocean, where we played in the waves near the Santa Monica Pier.

The girls and I had a fabulous time at the conference and in LA because I made sure that we stayed out of the dangerous neighborhoods, while guiding them to wonderful attractions and educational experiences.

Touring MySpace is a lot like touring Los Angeles. That is why I want to help you become familiar with MySpace the same way you become familiar with a major metropolitan area you visit as a tourist. A good place to go as the first stop in such situations is to a visitor's center.

▷ Your Visitor's Center Is Located at www.MySpace.com

The website address *www.myspace.com* is the home page for MySpace. (This is not to be confused with an individual's home page on MySpace, which contains a personal profile.) The MySpace home page is open to anyone, a place to welcome visitors and help them learn about their options during their visit to MySpace. MySpace.com provides a connection to pretty much any part of the entire MySpace metaphorical "metro area." Whatever *it* is you want to get to on MySpace, you can get there from the home page.

This "visitor's center" has lots of flashing advertisements, lots to draw your attention here and there, cool new people, hot new videos, attractive fashions, or ads for the latest TV show. Don't be distracted and definitely don't click on anything flashing that tells you *Congratulations! You've Won* ... whatever. Instead, look for what you need to become familiar with on MySpace for your teen's sake. To do this, I'll point out some helpful resources available here that should be of interest to any parent of a teen.

On the MySpace home page you will see a Member Login box, where members can enter their email address and password to get into their profile page and access their network of "friends," or where new people can sign up to become members. If your teen has a MySpace page, this is where they enter in, using their user email address and password. For now, just note where this is and what it is for; you don't need to go there yet and may not need to if you choose not to enter into MySpace for yourself.

Experience It Online!

If you want to get the full experience, you can go to *www.MySpace.com/momsanddads* and check my blog for this chapter. There you can find out how you can try out on MySpace what I am describing here. I'll show you how to locate each item mentioned below and experience it on MySpace. If you want to go the noncomputer route, you can read what I have written for you in the remainder of the chapter.

Your MySpace Interests Box

Visitor's centers always have a rack filled with lots of different brochures for restaurants, attractions, lodging, and so forth; whatever is available in their area for tourists is represented with a brochure. MySpace has something that functions like the brochure rack. It's a box that has titles of things that might interest you that you can get to by clicking on the word in the Interests box. The day I checked it to write this, the box included:

Books	Comedy	Jobs NEW!	MySpaceIM
Blogs	Filmmakers	Movies	Schools
ChatRooms	Games	Music	TV On Demand NEW!
Classifieds	Horoscopes	Music Videos	Videos

Just as brochures are changed seasonally, the items listed in this box change periodically. The day I checked it both "Jobs" and "TV on Demand" were highlighted as "New!" As MySpace expands, it will add new interests and perhaps drop others. Whatever is currently available in its virtual metro area will be found in the MySpace collection of interests. There's plenty to explore on MySpace even without becoming a member.

Let me start by showing you some of what's available through a few of the items listed in the Interests box. In doing so I hope to give you an idea of how this works and of the countless possibilities MySpace opens up for your teen. If you are already familiar with surfing the Web, this will come as no surprise to you. If you're not, you might be surprised at how handy the internet can be.

Let's say that we are interested in finding a movie showing in our area. We click on "Movies" from the Interests box. A new screen appears displaying all kinds of interesting information about current movies: top ten box-office hits, promotional trailers, featured films. There I also find a box titled: "Find Movie Showtimes and Tickets."

On that page I find a place where I can type in the movie I'd like to see, if I know. If I do that and click "Go," it will list everywhere that film is playing in my area (which I also typed in).

If I don't know which movie I'd like to see, the box titled "Find Movie Showtimes and Tickets" also has an option to just type in my area. If I do so and click "go," a new screen appeared listing all the theaters in my area, all the movies playing at each theater, and all the showtimes. This page also gives me the option to click on the trailers if I want to see previews of the movies. All of that comes through that one "virtual brochure" in the form of the word Movies in the MySpace. com Interests box.

I've only showed you one of the sixteen options in the Interests box. You can check out the possibilities on any of these that attract your attention and find many opportunities related to that topic. The TV on Demand option lets you watch episodes of your favorite Fox TV shows. The Blog option lets you search through columns where people are writing about whatever is on their minds. By choosing a category listed under Blogs and a keyword (I chose Religion & Philosophy for my category and Christian for my keyword), you can find out what others are thinking and writing about in weblogs on topics of interest to you.

Those are just a few of the "brochures" in the Interests box and how each can lead you to entirely different experiences, attractions, people, and neighborhoods. There's much more you or your teen could explore from this virtual visitor's center. This may help us understand why teens could spend hours on MySpace and what they might be doing.

Information for Parents Available at the MySpace.com Home Page

Let's turn our attention away from the Interests box and look for the kind of information that may be of most interest to you as a parent considering MySpace as an option for your teen. This information should be found at the bottom of the MySpace home page and will include a menu of important information about MySpace. It's a menu of options designed to familiarize visitors with the basics of MySpace. Remember, you don't have to be a MySpace member to access this information. This list of options looks like this:

About | FAQ | Terms | Privacy | Safety Tips | Contact MySpace | Promote! | Advertise | MySpace International
©2003-2006 MySpace.com. All Rights Reserved.

Here's a brief description of what you'll find among these choices:

About

This is a brief description of MySpace, who it's for, and how to use it.

FAQ: Frequently Asked Questions

This page has organized the most frequently asked questions about MySpace so they are easy for you to access. They're organized by "Top 6 Questions" and "Getting Started," along with lists of questions under the following categories:

Artist/Band Questions
Groups
Media Inquiry
Other
Profile Design
Reporting Abuse
Site Errors
Your Account

As with most things at MySpace, this listing will change as the questions frequently asked of them change. Questions are highlighted under each category. If you click on the question, you will be taken to the answer.

Most of the questions you have about MySpace can be answered from the FAQ link at the bottom of the MySpace home page. In each case, when you follow a link from the home page to another page, you should be able to return to the MySpace.com home page by clicking on MySpace.com in the upper left corner of that secondary page.

Terms

MySpace.com outlines the Terms of Use that all members and users are bound to comply with. Members must agree to these terms before being allowed to join. Violating these Terms of Use is grounds to have MySpace delete the user's account and their profile page. For your convenience, I've copied passages of particular interest to parents of teens here. If you want to read the entire legal document, you can do so by going online.

Please choose carefully the information you post on MySpace. com and that you provide to other Users. Your MySpace.com profile may not include the following items: telephone numbers, street addresses, last names, and any photographs containing nudity, or obscene, lewd, excessively violent, harassing, sexually explicit or otherwise objectionable subject matter. Despite this prohibition, information provided by other MySpace.com Members (for instance, in their Profile) may contain inaccurate, inappropriate, offensive or sexually explicit material, products or services, and MySpace. com assumes no responsibility or liability for this material. If you become aware of misuse of the MySpace Services by any person, please contact MySpace or click on the "Report Inappropriate Content" link at the bottom of any MySpace.com page.

MySpace.com may delete any Content that in the sole judgment of MySpace.com violates this Agreement or which may be offensive, illegal or violate the rights, harm, or threaten the safety of any person. MySpace.com assumes no responsibility for monitoring the MySpace Services for inappropriate Content or conduct. If at any time MySpace.com chooses, in its sole discretion, to monitor the MySpace Services, MySpace.com nonetheless assumes no responsibility for the Content, no obligation to modify or remove any inappropriate Content, and no responsibility for the conduct of the User submitting any such Content.[1]

There is a long list of the kinds of activities and content that is prohibited and another list of activities and content that is illegal and will be investigated and turned over to law enforcement authorities. If you don't want to read the entire legal document in the Terms of Use section, it is advisable to go over the lists of prohibited and illegal activities with your teen. Many of them make for good discussion starters and might even someday keep someone from being arrested or interrogated by the Secret Service!

Privacy

This page summarizes the privacy policy and practices of MySpace, including this statement: "MySpace.com cares deeply about online privacy. If you have any questions concerning this privacy policy, please email us at privacy@MySpace.com."

On the Privacy page you'll find sections covering:

Information Collection and Use by MySpace
Invitations and Other Communications to Non-members
Use of Cookies
Links
Chat Rooms, Journals, and WebLogs, Message Boards, Classifieds, and Public Forums
Correcting/Updating or Removing Information
Email Choice/Opt out
Third Party Advertising
Sharing and Disclosure of Information MySpace.com Collects
Changes in Privacy Policy
Contacting the Website[2]

Safety Tips

Here you will find safety tips for MySpace users and their parents. I will cover these areas in chapter 14, "Basic Safety Tips for MySpace."

Contact MySpace

This page says, "Questions, Comments, Concerns? We'd like to hear from you," followed by a box where you can choose from a drop-down list of topics and subtopics. There is also a reminder to check the Frequently Asked Questions.

Promote

This page gives MySpace members a way to promote MySpace on their website. This requires uploading images and copying code — which are still actions I turn to my teens to have done. Besides, for most parents reading this book, the jury is still out on MySpace. So it's not likely that promoting it will top our to-do list.

Advertise

This is a form to advertise a product or service on MySpace.com.

MySpace International

Yes, MySpace is international! (Remember my page in German?) At the time of this writing MySpace had a global site, along with sites in Australia, France, Germany, Ireland, United Kingdom, and in the USA, but they are expanding.

◄◄ ►►

This concludes our perusal of the information about MySpace that you can reach from the visitor's center at the home page of MySpace.com. There are also helpful links to allow you to explore how to do the things MySpace "tourists" are often interested in. These include:

- Get Started on MySpace.
- Create Your Profile.
- Browse Through Profiles. (For our purposes, please don't browse now. It will distract you from your aim of understanding *your teen's* experience of MySpace and may take you to negative material that you don't need to see and that has nothing to do with your teen.)
- Invite Your Friends.

We will get to these activities later in the context of your teen's life and development. For now, I'm just making you aware that these options are available to access from the MySpace.com home page.

▷ Ask Yourself

1. What surprised you most about your visit to the MySpace metaphorical metro area?

   _____

   _____

2. What areas of interest or information do you want to go back to later to learn more?

   _____

   _____

   _____

3. What did you learn that you want to share with your teen, your spouse, or your group?

   _____

   _____

   _____

   _____

▷ Ask Your Teen

Use the following questions to find out more about your teen. For more fun, answer the same for yourself and compare notes with your teen.

1. Below is the interest box on MySpace. What three topics most interest you? Circle them.

Books	Comedy	Jobs NEW!	MySpaceIM
Blogs	Filmmakers	Movies	Schools
ChatRooms	Games	Music	TV On Demand NEW!
Classifieds	Horoscopes	Music Videos	Videos

2. Why do those subjects interest you?

   _____

   _____

   _____

6

How to Find What You Are Searching For

May 1989 was a memorable month for me; that is when my son, Taylor, was born. That was a special month for Stephanie Lovatos too. I have never met her, but I read that she also gave birth that same month to her daughter Celina. Stephanie was living in Maui with her boyfriend, Celina's father, to whom she was not married. The three of them lived together in Maui until 1991, when Stephanie decided to move to California with her then two-year-old daughter.

Getting settled wasn't easy for Stephanie. When she could not find suitable living arrangements for herself and Celina, she asked the little girl's father (her former boyfriend) if he would take care of Celina in Maui while Stephanie got settled. He agreed. While Stephanie was searching for a suitable home for herself and her daughter, her ex married and moved away with his wife and Celina. When Stephanie came back to claim her daughter, she was unable to find any trace of her.

Stephanie immediately sought out authorities, who told her that without the benefit of marriage, neither she nor her former boyfriend had legal custody. Therefore the police could not help her. They suggested she search for her daughter on her own. She searched through all channels she could think of—searched and searched, year in and year out for fifteen years. How different those months of May each year must have been for her. While I was having birthday parties with Taylor, she was sadly commemorating another year without her daughter. She was wondering where she was, what she was doing to celebrate another year of life, what she looked like, whether she knew her mother still loved her and was still looking for her.

Stephanie was told her best bet was to try to find her daughter on her own, but she kept running into dead ends. She later explained,

"Back then, obviously there was no internet or anything like that." Her search was fruitless and frustrating until 2006, when she hit on the idea of using MySpace. She had heard news reports about the site being popular with teens, and Celina would be seventeen by then. She hoped it might be able to help her find her long-lost daughter. In February Stephanie had someone create a MySpace page for her. She didn't know enough to do it on her own, but that was not going to stand in her way! On her personal profile page where it asked "Who would you like to meet?" she wrote:

> Who I'd like to meet: Celina Aquire
> If you ever see this, I have not seen you since you were two. I have been looking for you all this time. Get a hold of me. I have important information to tell you.

Then Stephanie waited and hoped. Four months passed without reply. On June 14, 2006, Stephanie was contacted by a cousin with whom she had lost touch. Her cousin explained that she had found Stephanie using MySpace search functions. This made Stephanie realize she might be able to do the same to search for her daughter, Celina.

Within minutes—*minutes*—Stephanie had found her daughter Celina's page. She told *CBS News*, "I kept thinking, twenty minutes on a ... website, after fifteen years of phone calls and searching." That's what it took for her to find her daughter. Can you imagine how she felt as she looked at her daughter's MySpace profile page? Once she found Celina's MySpace page, she discovered she was living in Florida with her father. It took the intervention of Stephanie's best friend and Celina's boyfriend—who made her MySpace page—and some explaining (since Celina's father had raised her to believe that his wife was her mother, until she found her birth certificate when she was thirteen), but a phone call was arranged.

Stephanie said, "Celina, this is Mom."

Lovato recalls, "I started to choke up, and said, 'Look, hear me out, don't hang up. I just—you need to know—I never abandoned you. You were taken from me. No one has ever let me know where you are. The past fifteen years, I've never given up. I've looked for you. I love you and I miss you." In early July Stephanie and Celina embraced, reunited at the San Francisco airport after fifteen long years apart. As I looked at the photo and video clip of their interview from *The Early Show*, it brought tears to my eyes. There was Stephanie sitting beside Celina, the two of them looking so much alike.

Celina said of their reunion, "It's been an amazing time for me. I never thought this day would happen, and it's just wonderful to be sitting next to her right now." Stephanie found her daughter thanks to MySpace.

Parents Looking for Teen's MySpace Profile

Most parents I meet aren't going into MySpace looking for their teen's profile page in the same way Stephanie was looking. Most parents I know who are learning to search MySpace are looking to discover if their teen has a MySpace page—perhaps against the wishes of Mom and Dad. If so, when they find it, their "Aha!" moment may be more of a "Gotcha!" moment.

I am going to show you how to search for and find your teen's MySpace profile page or pages. However, before I do, I want to ask you to do something. Please go in searching to find *your son or daughter*, not just their MySpace page. Before you react—especially if they have not felt comfortable letting you know they have a page or if they have disobeyed your orders to not have a MySpace page—take a deep breath and first look at their page to see *the person*.

If your teen has gone behind your back to make a MySpace profile, you will need to deal with that disobedience. Before you do, though, take in the wonder of the *person* who is expressing his or her life, friendships, interests, and style. With that said, let me share with you how you can most simply find your teen's profile, if he or she has one. If you need to go beyond this, ask someone who is familiar with MySpace to help you search further.

Searching through the Schools

The easiest way to track down the profile of a teen you know is to search through their school. MySpace has set up affiliations with over 29,000 schools to create MySpace school groups with a moderator who helps keep the interaction safe. When a teen sets up a profile, they are asked what school they attend or have attended. If they list that school, you will be able to find that profile by looking at all the profiles of teens who identify that school as the one they attend.

One word of warning: it's best to follow the instructions to go as directly as possible to your teen's profile page or those of their closest friends and classmates. If you start just browsing randomly through profiles of other students, you may get the wrong impression. Don't judge your teen's use of MySpace by what you may see from other students randomly selected from their school. You need to see who *your teen* associates with to have a fair view of what MySpace is in his or her experience. That is what you are searching for, isn't it? Here's one way to find their school:

Step 1: Go to *www.MySpace.com* and find the Interests box:

Books	Comedy	Jobs NEW!	MySpaceIM
Blogs	Filmmakers	Movies	Schools
ChatRooms	Games	Music	TV On Demand NEW!
Classifieds	Horoscopes	Music Videos	Videos

Step 2: Click on Schools. You'll see a box on that page that looks something like this:

Schools

Find Your School

School Name

Country

State/Province/Territory

Find

Step 3: Type in the name of your teen's school, the country, and the state/province/territory, then click the Find button.

There are times when you will encounter a notice, "Sorry, we've encountered an error." If so, try back later. One of the good things about using MySpace is that it does develop patience and persistence, both good character qualities. But when this three-step process works, a list of schools should appear. If your teen's school is listed, click on the school's name. If your teen's school name is not listed, there will be a box titled "Find Your School" and under that is the phrase "Can't find your school?" Follow the instructions there and you should be able to find it.

Schools

Schools matching "Natomas Charter School" in California, UNITED STATES

Natomas Charter #19
Sacramento, United States

Find Your School

Can't find your school?

Choose a city from the list to view all schools in that city:

City/Town

Find

Try a new search.

Natomas Charter School

United States

California

Find

Or submit your school to get it added to the list.

Another Way to Search for Their School

If this approach doesn't work for you, there is another way to find your teen's school. You may want to try this:

Step 1: Point your cursor up to the top right of the screen; search options are up there.

Step 2: Click on "MySpace" above the Search box, and the Search button may change to read "Search MySpace."

Step 3: Type in the name of your teen's school, with or without the city and state.

Step 4: Hit *search* and presto! You may find a list of thumbnail photos or at least a list of highlighted user names of students from that school. These should be the profiles of every student who claims to go to or be alumni of your teen's school.

Step 5: If you get this far, scroll through these photos or user names looking for someone you know to be a close friend of your teen. The user names are rarely the real names of students, but if your daughter is a dancer and you see *www.myspace.com/dancersrock* as a screen name, that may take you to the profile page of another student dedicated to dance.

Step 6: You may need to click on "Next" highlighted at the bottom of the list to find more students. Many schools have hundreds of MySpace profiles, so you may need to spend some time looking. It's not fair to judge your teen by some of the photos or user names that may be inappropriate if that person is not someone with whom your teen associates. There are bound to be a few bad apples in every basket.

Step 7: Once you've found someone you know to be a close friend of your teen, or maybe even your teen, you can click on the photo or the highlighted user name, and you will be taken to their profile page.

Step 8: Once you arrive at the profile page of a friend of your teen, look for the section that lists their "friends" with accompanying photos. If your teen has a MySpace page, he or she will be among the friends listed by their closest real-life friends.

▷ Find Your Teen by Name or Email

Don't be discouraged if you weren't able to find your teen's page through the school listing. There is another way, besides the best which is to talk with your teen and have him show you his page. There is another way you can try.

Step 1: Go to *www.MySpace.com* and look for the menu bar that goes across the top of the page. Look for the word "Search" on that menu.

Step 2: Click on "Search" in this menu bar. This will bring up a search page that gives you the options.

To find someone you know:

Find Someone You Know

Find a Friend
Select search by: ⦿ Name ◯ Display Name ◯ Email

Taylor Neal [Find]
Example: Tom Jones or Tom or tjones@hotmail.com

To find a classmate:

Find Your Classmates

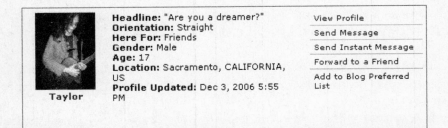

Step 3: Using the "Find a Friend" option, select whether to search by name or by email address, then type in that information. I searched using my son's name "Taylor Neal." Several came up, but among them I found his photo and profile.

If this doesn't turn up results it may be that your teen doesn't have a MySpace profile. (That's not to say your teen isn't on another social networking site you are not aware exists.)

However you find your way to your teen's profile page or profile brief, you may need some help deciphering what you find. On the day I found Taylor's profile brief it looked like this:

Taylor

Headline: "Are you a dreamer?"
Orientation: Straight
Here For: Friends
Gender: Male
Age: 17
Location: Sacramento, CALIFORNIA, US
Profile Updated: Dec 3, 2006 5:55 PM

View Profile

Send Message

Send Instant Message

Forward to a Friend

Add to Blog Preferred List

This gives me lots of information. I will decipher this to help you understand how to read your teen's profile should you find it.

The picture is the default photo your teen has chosen—at the moment—to represent his profile. Taylor's is a photo of him with his beloved guitar.

The profile tells his **first name, age, gender, and the city** he lives in (I'm going to talk to Taylor about taking that bit of information off as it is not needed and could lead a predator to our door).

"Are you a dreamer?" is the headline he has chosen. Teens change headlines frequently, but the headline they choose says a lot about how they are representing themselves to the world.

The section "... this holiday life fans, Natomas Charter, Charter Pride '07 [designating his graduating class], Euphoric (U4IC)" is a list of groups he has affiliated himself with on MySpace.

Children: Someday

Education: High School

Occupation: Ebay

These are all the answers he has given to basic questions about himself. ***www.MySpace.com/dinopirate*** is the URL for this MySpace profile (he has a separate URL for his music page).

Groups:	this holiday life fans, Natomas Charter, Charter Pride 07, Euphoric (U4IC), Remembering Brian, Red-Heads Unite, NCS Drama Department, BLAKE ATTACK! View All Taylor's Groups

I happen to know that the word "dinopirate" has special meaning, coming from his favorite book, *The Pirates! In an Adventure with Scientists*, which is the only book currently listed under books on this profile page. As you are searching, remember every choice your teen makes, including the URL, may hold meaning and may reveal something interesting about him or his interests.

When you find the profile page, you may want to go over the information your teen is posting to help him or her decide what information may need to be removed or changed later for safety reasons. But for now, look to find *your son or daughter*.

▷ What Are You Searching For?

You can also search MySpace for long-lost cousins, the way Stephanie Lovato's cousin searched for her. In the past you might look in the phone directory to see if you could locate that friend, but MySpace gives you far greater reach to find people almost anywhere if they have a MySpace connection.

I was recently contacted by a friend from high school whom I haven't seen in almost thirty years. It was exciting, and weird, to get a message calling me by my maiden name and asking if it was me. She and I have caught up without even speaking by taking a quick tour of each other's lives through the profile and photos of families on our pages. We've also sent each other email and become "friends" on MySpace, as we used to be in the drama department at our high school. I think she found me by going back to my high school's MySpace page, where I am listed among the alumni. Once you start searching, you realize that you can search for people, old songs, musical artists in various genres, and so on.

▷ Experience It Online!

If you want to get the full experience of MySpace.com, you can go to *www.MySpace.com/momsanddads* and check my blog for this chapter. There you can find out how you can try out what I am describing here on MySpace. If you want to go the noncomputer route, continue reading what I have written for you in the remainder of the chapter.

▷ A Basic Way to Find People, Music, and Videos on MySpace

If you've opted to follow along on the computer, get back to *www. MySpace.com* and follow along. If not, I'll describe it for you. In the top band of the MySpace home page, from about the center toward the right corner, you'll see a blank box with a button to the right that says Search. Above the blank box you will see the options of things you can search, including Web | MySpace | People | Music | Blogs | Video.

These options too are subject to change, but the basic search function should remain the same. One of the search options will be highlighted. Whichever is highlighted, that word will fill in the blank in the search button. So if "Web" is highlighted, the search button may read, "Search Web." *Web* refers to the World Wide Web, which includes MySpace and thousands of other websites as well, giving you a much broader range for your search. If "MySpace" is highlighted, the button may change to read "Search MySpace," and it will limit your search to things and people on MySpace. If you highlight People, Music, Blogs, or Videos, you will be looking for those things *within MySpace*.

Searching for People

Let's suppose you wanted to see if an old friend of yours has a MySpace profile. You can search MySpace or People (but if your friend is being cautious, he or she may not be using the correct name, or you might not know that person's married name). You will find a list of profiles that may come close to referring to the person you have named. You can then scroll through them and perhaps find your long-lost friend. If that doesn't work, type in the name of your old high school or college with the city, then look through the people who have listed themselves as alumni. Who knows whom you might find!

Searching for Music

Let's say that your friend (me) told you about her son's acoustic music that she'd like you to hear. You could try to find his music by searching from the MySpace home page in various ways. First, point your cursor toward the very top of the *www.MySpace.com* home page search box and look for "Music," then click on it. The Search button will change to read "Search Music" (this is music found within MySpace). You can type in the kind of music you're seeking—say "acoustic"—and click "Search Music." You'd see that 110 pages full of various music artists have listed themselves as "acoustic." After I scrolled through ten of these pages, even I—Taylor's mother—decided it wasn't worth the effort to search that way.

Then I noticed a box at the top of the page I was taken to when I clicked "Search Music" (and each following page) that said: "Set Search Criteria." There I discovered I could click the arrow next to "Genre" and choose from a drop-down menu of more styles of music than I knew existed; or I could search by band name (or related items on that drop-down menu), or by keyword. (Hint: if you know a specific keyword, like a person's name, go there first; the more specific, the better when you're trying to search effectively.) Since I've told you my son's name is Taylor Neal, you should be able to type Taylor Neal into the keyword box. Then click the Update button, and you will see something that looks about like this:

| Home | Browse | Search | Invite | Film | Mail | Blog | Favorites | Forum | Groups | Events | Videos | Music | Comedy | Classifieds |

MYSPACE MUSIC   Music Videos | Directory | Search | Top Artists | Shows | Music Forums | Music Classifieds | Artist Signup

Music » Search Results

Locate This Person   Sponsored Links
Current address and phone available. Instant results.
www.usa-people-search.com

Page 1 of 1

Taylor Neal   Plays: 4,178
Genre: Blues / Folk Rock / Acoustic   Views: 2,719
Location: Sacramento, California   Fans: 375
Last Update: Nov 22, 2006

Page 1 of 1

Set Search Criteria

Genre: Any Genre
Search By: Select
Keyword: Taylor Neal
Location: United States
            ○ California
            ⊙ Any ▾ miles of 95843
Sort By: ○ Plays   ○ Friends
            ○ New   ⊙ Alphabetical

                              Update

There he is! If you then click on his photo or name, you will be taken to his band profile page, where you can sample up to four of his original songs (I don't mind if you do). My mom, his homebound grandma, loves this feature because she can hear her "Sweetie" singing anytime she wants.

While I was playing around with this search, I tried looking under "Folk Rock" but didn't find anything listed there. I had to look around a bit (and I sort of know what I'm doing). This is common. So I suggest you approach this as a *fun* search, sort of like an Easter egg hunt. You kind of know what you're looking for, but you may find some great things you weren't expecting that are slight variations on what you were specifically looking for along the way. That's part of the fun of MySpace (especially for music lovers who want to sample new artists in a genre they enjoy and one reason people can spend hours on MySpace).

Searching for Videos

Let's look at another example of how to find something that may interest you or your teen. Let's say that I am your friend and I want to show you this really funny video clip I've heard about. I was told that some time ago *Saturday Night Live* aired a comedy sketch about setting up a MySpace page, a mom, and creepy predators. I thought you and your teen might find it both funny and instructional (and, yes a bit horrifying for us parents), so I wanted to see if I could show you how to find it so you could see it for yourself. Knowing that MySpace has a link to Videos in the Interests box, I decided to check to see if I could find it there.

Here's how I did it. At the Interests box I clicked on Videos, and a new screen came up. I found where it said "Search Videos" with a blank box next to it. Inside the blank box I typed: "SNL Sketch How to Create a MySpace Profile" (I had to try a few different descriptive phrases before I found the one that led to what I was looking for). Then I clicked on the "Search Videos" button.

Presto! A new screen came up showing two thumbnail images of screen shots from the video and the link said "How to Create a MySpace." Yes, that's the one I want to share with you!

Here is where the appeal of MySpace becomes apparent. I really *do* want to share that skit with you and your teen. I can tell you about it, but there's no adequate substitute for sketch comedy. To get the full effect, you must see the sketch. If you or your teen repeats the steps I have just described, you could see it for yourself.

Here's how: Click on the photo or title of the sketch, and if you have DSL or a high-speed Internet connection, it will play the video of the sketch for you on your computer. I highly recommend watching this! You'll laugh, and your teen will learn about sexual predators and deception on MySpace without your having to say a word.

When you get done watching the video, all you have to do to be transported back to the MySpace home page (or visitor's center to us) is to scroll all the way to the top of the page, point your cursor toward the top left corner, and you'll see MySpace.com/Help/Sign Out.

Click on MySpace.com and it will take you back to the MySpace.com home page, which is where you want to be.

What If We Accidentally Find Something Bad While Searching?

Remember, searching MySpace should be fun, filled with curiosity and genuine interest on your part. However, there is a chance that you may accidentally venture into pages or "neighborhoods" that are offensive, make you uncomfortable, or seem inappropriate or dangerous. If that happens, you need to get out of that page immediately, the same way you would if you made a wrong turn into a scary neighborhood in real life.

Here's how you do it: Scroll to the top left of whatever MySpace page you are on and click on MySpace.com. If you somehow get to a page that doesn't have that option showing, the toolbar of your Internet browser should have a "back" button or a "home" option; click one of those and go to a page that has the MySpace.com option. Then click on MySpace.com and you should be taken back to the MySpace home page. If you ever get to a page where you can't find one of those options, you can exit the Web altogether by clicking the "x" in the top right corner. Then you can start over and go back to *www.MySpace.com* if you like.

▷ What We Search for Says a Lot about Us

Knowing that you have the power to find almost anything you can think of opens up a world of imagination. When we reveal what we would search for, we reveal to our teens much about ourselves. When our teens dare to share what they would search for with us, they in turn reveal much about themselves. If our teens feel safe and assured that we will not penalize them or denigrate them, they just may open up and show us what they would search for on MySpace.

▷ Ask Your Teen

Use the following questions to find out more about your teen. For more fun, answer the same for yourself and compare notes with your teen.

1. What would you choose to search for first on the MySpace.com search bar (circle one)?

   People | Music | Blogs | Video | Film | Books | Events | Groups

2. Why would that be your first choice?

   _____

   _____

3. Is there someone or something that you would like to try to find using MySpace? Who/What is it?

   _____

   _____

4. If we were to go to the Search Music section and drop down the list of music genres, which three would you pick first to search? (If you don't know how to get back there, your teen can probably take you there. Otherwise, just leave the question open to having your teen list their three favorite music genres.)

   _____

   _____

   _____

   _____

5. Could you help me find that video of the *Saturday Night Live* MySpace sketch and watch it with me?

If we can start sharing what we are searching for, our varying tastes in music, and a few laughs with our teens, we'll be better able to discuss the important issues related to life as well as MySpace.

We've already looked at some general reasons teens love MySpace. In the next section we are going to learn more specifically how teens use MySpace to do what teens have always done, only in exciting new ways. Along the way, we'll discuss some of the safety issues raised by those activities and begin to look at ways to minimize the risks. But I will save my final explanation on safety for later in the book, when you have a better understanding of how teens tend to use MySpace.

Part 3

How Teens
Use MySpace

Communicating with Friends and Peers on MySpace

Toward the end of last summer, my daughter Haley heard from a friend that a boy she had been friends with in seventh grade, Timmy, had died in a drowning accident. She was deeply saddened at his reported death, but she wasn't sure the rumor was true. In our area there are drowning accidents every spring and summer, and Timmy's first and last names were common.

While I searched through traditional channels, Haley went to MySpace and started networking with her friends. She was quickly convinced that the rumor was true and her friend had indeed died. I went to the school and asked the administrators and teachers who had known Timmy when he attended that school if they knew anything about the reports. No one there had heard anything about it. I asked them to check the MySpace sites, but those sites were blocked from the school.

Next I turned to our local newspaper and finally found an obituary that confirmed Haley's sad conclusion. Long before we adults even knew this sad and important information, Haley and her other friends who knew Timmy were commemorating him, eulogizing, comforting each other, and even sharing prayers for his family via MySpace and the internet. This convinced me of the power of MySpace for communicating with peers

One of the basic uses of MySpace is the variety of ways one can communicate with friends and peers. This has always been standard fare with teens, so if you want to know what your teen is doing on MySpace, you should know the basics about how they communicate with each other on the site. I'm not trying to teach you all the ins and outs of how to use the communication functions for yourself; there are other ways you can learn that. Here we are focusing on your teen and the possibilities that MySpace presents in the context of how adolescents communicate.

As parents we must concern ourselves not just with the functions of *how* our teens communicate; we need to concern ourselves with *what* they communicate, with *whom* they communicate, how they *treat people*, and how others who communicate with them are *treating them*. That is our focus in this chapter.

We will also look at what it means to be a "friend" on MySpace and what a real friend is, and we must help our teens consider whom they accept and decline as their friend on a social networking site. I'll explain the privileges afforded "friends" and how to manage them on MySpace, including screening, choosing/accepting, inviting, declining, and ranking them. As parents we need to help our teens work through how they treat people they call "friend" online and off, and what criteria they can use to block someone who is not behaving as a friend.

The Basic Forms of Communication on MySpace

Here too I will connect the unfamiliar buzz words and communication tools of MySpace to familiar forms of communication. The primary means of communication on MySpace include: Mail (email), IM (Instant Messaging), Bulletins, and Comments. These can only be used by MySpace members. Let's compare these to things we know. (See table on page 77.)

Privileges Given to "Friends" on MySpace

When someone is designated as a "friend" on a MySpace profile, this gives that person special privileges. Such people will be able to access and view all parts of your personal profile, including your pics, videos, blogs (unless set so only you can read it as a diary), and comments. They can also leave comments on your personal profile page, your pictures, videos, and blogs. They will also receive any bulletins you send or any event invitations designated to be sent to your friends. You will receive notice of any bulletins they send to all of their friends.

Your "friends" will also be able to click on the icons of your other friends and access their profiles (unless they have their account set to

Familiar Form of Communication	is like	MySpace Form of Communication
Passing private notes; kids and teens have been passing notes since they could write. Notes are meant for a particular person but can be shown to others by the recipient.		**Mail** on MySpace is the same as email. This is also the same as **Send Message.**
Talking to someone from another room; you can't see each other, but you're talking in real time.		**IM** or **Instant Messaging** on MySpace. These are real-time text messages that can be sent back and forth by the computer in real time, showing up on the screen. You can opt to block all IMs or only get IMs from friends on your MySpace friends list.
A message board on a dorm room door in a public hallway. College students often put up a message board on the outside of their dorm room door. That way anyone who stops by can leave a message or comment to be read when that person returns to the room. Since anyone passing by can read the notes, that influences what is written. If they don't like what someone leaves on their board they can take it down as soon as they see it.		**Comments** on MySpace; anyone who has access to your teen's profile page can read the comments left by their friends. Only friends can leave comments. They can leave comments on blogs or pictures or the profile page. MySpace Comments go beyond text to include the options of music, video, and pictures. The user can take down anything they don't like or even opt to screen all comments before they are posted (but that's sort of a hassle).
Distributing a flier or putting an insert in a church bulletin allows the one communicating to get the same message to a specific group of people. It is available to all but each one can choose whether to read it.		**Post a Bulletin** on MySpace. Users can send one message to all their friends. The title will show up for their friend, who may or may not choose to read it.

private). Therefore, a MySpace user should review their list of friends periodically. If anyone is not living up to the privileges of being on that list or is someone you would not want to receive your bulletins or event invitations, you can remove them from the complete friend list by "de-selecting" them (and they will not be notified this has happened).

Limiting the Friends List

The best way to make communicating via MySpace safe is for your teen to limit who can communicate with him or her on MySpace and who receives their bulletins. This is done primarily by limiting the "friends" list. Conceivably, you could set up a MySpace account with the safest settings and limit the "friends" to just you and your teen (or you, your spouse, and your teen). That way communication is limited to your very small group. This can also work for small groups at school and church too. As long as the list of "friends" is limited to friends or associates whom you trust in real life, communication on MySpace is far more protected than if the friends list is inflated with anyone and everyone who asks to be your teen's friend.

Experience It Online!

The best way to learn about communication on MySpace is to communicate with your teen *on* MySpace while communicating *about* MySpace. I invite you to go to *www.MySpace.com/momsanddads*, where I will show you how to set up your MySpace account and your teen's, step by step. Check the blog associated with this chapter. I'll show you how to make all the settings private so you can communicate with each other and only each other for now, to get the hang of what I describe in the book. Invite your teen to be your "friend" on your new page, and make it clear his or her page is also to be set to the same account settings as yours, private.

Real-Life Friends and Peers Break into Tribes

· Probably the most basic use for MySpace is to connect and communicate with friends and peers, but teens are selective in their own way. For ages teens have found their group or clique or tribe within the larger social order. This is part of how they develop their identity. Remember when you were in high school? The band kids ate lunch in the band room, the drama club sat near the theater, the football players and cheerleaders had their places staked out, the stoners knew where they were to meet their group, as did the science geeks, and so on.

Likewise, today's teens know whom they associate with, where their group sits at lunch, and what their group considers acceptable dress and hairstyle. They know whom they feel comfortable associating with and whom they would never care to associate themselves with. Without being told, every student body on any campus in America will divide themselves up into groups. There are some individuals who are accepted and comfortable in several groups. But most people know with whom they are expected to associate at lunch.

Where Does Your Teen "Sit" on MySpace?

"Tribes" form on social networking sites in similar fashion to the way they form on junior and senior high school campuses. This is why it is not fair to your teen to decide that you are going to "browse" MySpace to see what's going on and decide from whatever you happen to stumble into that you think it is or is not appropriate for your teen to be on MySpace. That is like saying that you were going to check out their school but happened to enter campus where the stoners and smokers hang out—where your teen would never consider going—and then declaring that the school is not a good place because of what you saw there. How good or bad a teen's MySpace experience (not unlike their high school experience) is has a great deal to do with *who* their friends are and whom they allow to associate with their group.

If you have seen things on MySpace that are offensive—and there is plenty there that is—you may declare to your teen that you've decided it's not a good place. Their argument will likely be that *their friends* are not like that and that they have enough common sense to stay away from the bad places and people. The point we must understand is that your teen may have a better grasp on this than most of us parents do.

The best way to resolve such a conflict—which is a conflict in many homes—is to take a metaphorical "campus visit" together. We need to see what MySpace is for our teen. The best way to get a sense of that is to visit the people and places they would choose to visit if allowed to use MySpace. If your teen seems indignant and offended when you bring up the unsavory neighborhoods and activities that go on and are recorded on MySpace, it may be because your teen would never choose to associate himself with such people and activities.

Our lack of understanding regarding how MySpace functions as an intertwined network of smaller tribes or communities may contribute to frustration as we argue with our teen. What MySpace is to your teen may be very different from what you think it is or what we have seen for ourselves (remember the blind men and the elephant?).

We're Looking for a Few Good "Friends"

Even in the process of signing up for MySpace, your teen is encouraged to invite her "friends" to join her on MySpace. A person joining MySpace can automatically invite everyone in the address books for their various email accounts outside of MySpace. If they click on yes, those people will be sent an invitation by email. This is why your teen may be receiving invitations to join regularly. It can boost the ego of a teen to see that they have lots and lots of friends. Since anyone coming to their profile page can see a number telling how many "friends" they have, this has its appeal.

It's our job as parents to help our teen think of this in a different way (especially because everyone who is granted the status of "friend" has access to your teen's profile, receives bulletins, and can see the other's content). It is also important because the impression one gets of your teen on their MySpace page comes partially from the images projected by their friends and the kind of material posted by them.

The Bible says that there is a definite connection between a person's heart (including character) and what comes out of their mouths—in this case, the kinds of things they choose to post on MySpace. Discussing this presents a great opportunity for us to instruct and guide our teens to choose their friends on and off MySpace carefully according to how well their values mesh.

Remember the old recruiting slogan of the US Marine Corps: *We're looking for a few good men?* That is the kind of attitude we need to advance with our teens regarding how they choose their MySpace "friends." We must guide them to be discriminating in the best sense of the word. These days the US Marines are recruiting on MySpace, but true to form they are concerned about the character and values of those who would associate themselves as a "friend" of the Marine Corps. Anyone wanting to be their friend will receive a pop-up message that says, "To be a Marine is always acting with honor, courage and commitment. We demand it of ourselves and we ask it of our friends." According to Lt. Col. Mike Zeliff, MCRC's top advertising officer, the pop-up message is a way to show potential recruits that they have to earn their standing with the Corps through the quality of their character.[1]

The Marines know the values and standards they are looking for in their friends. What are the standards and criteria your teen uses, or what you would have him use to screen friends? Below is a list of possible criteria one can use to select suitable "friends" for their MySpace page (duplicated so that you and your teen can circle what you deem most important). This list is just a sampling, but it will get you started thinking about this topic and help you and your teen come up with a list of *your agreed-upon* criteria.

The older your teens become, the less they will want your control over whom they choose as "friends." It is best to incorporate this kind of training while your teen is younger. Your teen wanting to be on MySpace gives you tremendous leverage when it comes to helping him learn to choose good friends. MySpace friends who meet your approval can be a condition for allowing him or her to be on MySpace.

Ask Your Teen

Circle the criteria you deem important for someone to be your MySpace "friend":

Teen's List	Parent's List
Friend in real life	Friend in real life
Classmate in real life	Classmate in real life
Trustworthy	Trustworthy
Funny	Funny
Popular	Popular
Attractive	Attractive
Does not use profane language	Does not use profane language
Similar taste in music	Similar taste in music

Teen's List	Parent's List
Does not post inappropriate content	Does not post inappropriate content
Reliable	Reliable
Supportive	Supportive
Encouraging	Encouraging
Not rude	Not rude
Kind	Kind

Take turns circling what you and your teen deem important in choosing a MySpace friend. You may want to share the advice given in *Seventeen* magazine's safety tips, designed for parents and teens:

Be Skeptical

We may have an idea of who someone is or why they're messaging us, but the truth is, when we're online we should be a little more skeptical. As you're connecting with people, get to know them first before adding them to your friends list. Only add the people that you want to see your profile, check out your friends and view your photos.[2]

There Are Friends and There Are MySpace "Friends"

What is a friend? Ask your teen that question and listen to the answer. People are thinking about that more these days, thanks to MySpace. Just because someone sends you an invitation to become a "friend" on their MySpace page does not make that person a real friend. We should remind our teens that as they move out into life, the friends they choose to ally themselves with will make a tremendous difference in the direction and quality of their lives.

The Bible says, "Do not be misled: 'Bad company corrupts good character'" (1 Corinthians 15:33), and "A man of many companions may come to ruin, but there is a friend who sticks closer than a brother" (Proverbs 18:24). We get to choose those whom we honor with the title of "friend," and those choices go a long way in shaping the course of our lives and the development or destruction of our character. Therefore, help your teen think through the appropriate criteria to use in order to accept or decline "friend" requests.

Practice Declining Friend Requests

If you are thinking about allowing your teen to join MySpace or any other social networking site, the best way to ensure the quality of that experience is to monitor their list of "friends" until your teen has demonstrated the ability to do this well. If you are coming in late and your teen already has a list of friends, some of whom you find questionable, it may be socially precarious to start deleting friends because they don't meet with Mom's or Dad's approval. Handle this with sensitivity — not only for your teen but also for the others who may be hurt by being deleted. Remember how fragile your ego was when you were that age.

To start out, you can insist on screening and giving approval before any new "friends" are added. If this is your approach, your teen will likely have to repeatedly decline others' requests to become a friend on MySpace. These requests are sent by email, and the person wanting to become a friend will be notified if their request is accepted or denied. If you limit your teen's friends to those you approve (which I recommend as you get started), he or she should have a few standard comments for declining the friend requests graciously.

With your teen, come up with a list of kind, or funny, or "blame the parents" options for declining friend requests if you plan to take this course. Here are some ideas to get you started:

Sorry, I'm only allowed to have one friend, my dog, Scruffy.
Sorry, no hard feelings, I hope. I'm limited to people I already
    know in real life.
Sorry, my "friend" card is filled at the moment.
Sorry, my mom read this book *MySpace for Moms and Dads*, so my
    friends are currently subject to parental approval.

Write a few options your teen finds suitable here:

_____

_____

_____

_____

We need to reassure our teens that it's not mean to decline a "friend" request. While we must be kind and respectful to every person, that doesn't mean we have to include them in our circle of friends. Discretion is a virtue that helps us keep our lives protected.

We must also bear in mind that when someone joins our circle of "friends" on MySpace, they will receive any bulletin we send that we may want only our real friends to see. We allow our real friends to peek into our lives, share our thoughts, and give input. That's important. While it's nice to have people want to be your friend, one must carefully consider the ramifications and be selective. Remember, we're looking for *a few good* friends.

Play the Golden Rule Game: What Kind of a Friend Are You?

This is a good time to talk about what it means to *be* a good friend to others as well. Your teen should carefully consider how he or she treats others on MySpace. Those whom we include in our list of "friends" should not be subject to hurtful jokes or online pranks that spread far and wide on the internet. Behind each email address or profile are real people who have feelings. Anything your teen says or does on MySpace will most likely make its way to many more people, including anyone being made fun of or talked about.

Remind your teen to play the Golden Rule game: Whatever you would have others do to you, do to them. Whatever you would not want someone to do to you, do not do to others. That goes for MySpace as it does for any other social networking site.

Cyber-bullying and harassment are some of the dangers associated with MySpace. Most parents worry that their teen might be the victim of such hurtful activities. We also need to worry that our teen might be the bully! The only way to find out is to monitor your teen's activity and make sure he or she will not participate in such hurtful behavior.

MySpace has consequences for inappropriate behavior on the site, including having the profile deleted. Decide in advance what the consequences would be if your teen's conduct and words on MySpace turned out to be hurtful to someone else. Hopefully, setting up the consequences in advance and discussing this issue will prevent it from happening. If every mom and dad monitored their teen to make sure that cyber-bullying and harassment didn't happen from their home, it would happen much less often. Let's all do our part.

Ranking Your Friends

Each MySpace profile page has a place for "friends." The default setting will show the top four or top eight friends on that person's list. In the socially competitive world of teens, this can create problems. Each person who is on someone else's "friends" list will be able to see where they are ranked. Putting people in a social pecking order is part of human experience, but the stark visual nature of the Top Eight or other ranking systems available on MySpace can hurt people's feelings. Some thought should be given to this if your teen is going to have a page, and we too should consider it if we are going to have a page.

I recently received this comment on my profile page from my daughter Haley:

Aug 12, 2006 2:36 AM

I see that Taylor is before me on your top 4! I see who the favorite is! And Casey's not even on there...

just joshin love you ma hope you have a most excellent day

Delete My Comment

To which I replied:

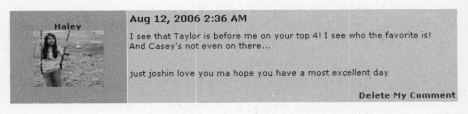

Aug 12, 2006 6:43 AM

Haley, you need not worry about your position on my top friends list, nor about my affection for Casey. There is no ranking for your mother's love! It is boundless and fierce. However, to clarify for those who might wonder; I will rotate your position with Taylor's regularly and announce that Casey does not participate in MySpace but I love her all the same. Thanks for Checking!

Delete My Comment

For his part, Taylor stays out of the fray altogether. He has chosen to fill his top "friends" with himself and bands he likes. That way, according to him, nobody gets hurt.

It is easy enough to change the top friends' settings. You can choose the top 4, 8, 12, 16, or 24. Whatever your teen chooses to do, this does require some thought or one might receive the kind of comment I received from Haley.

Who's Tom and Why Does He Think He's My Friend?

One need never worry that she will be friendless on MySpace. The moment you join you've got a friend! Tom. Tom is one of the two men who founded MySpace. He stays in contact with all MySpace members to provide updates. On my German MySpace page he showed up speaking German! That Tom is one talented guy.

Ask Your Teen

Take this time to determine how your teen routinely communicates with his friends online (if not through MySpace, how?), via telephone, or in person. Ask your teen to share their thoughts on these questions. You can discuss this face-to-face, or if you set up dual MySpace pages, you can write about these topics in messages or in your blog.

1. What criteria would you use to choose whether to let someone be a "friend" on your MySpace page?

_____

_____

_____

_____

_____

_____

2. What criteria do you use to choose your real friends in life?

_____

_____

_____

_____

_____

_____

3. Check to see if your teen realizes the privileges afforded to someone accepted as a "friend" on MySpace. (Do you remember? It's in this chapter.) Who would be your Top 4, 8, 16, 24?

_____

_____

_____

_____

_____

_____

_____

_____

_____

That pretty much covers the basics of how teens communicate with friends and peers on MySpace. Next we will turn our attention to the area of self-expression by teens on MySpace and the important role that plays in their lives.

8

Self-Expression on MySpace

Dr. Kathy Koch (pronounced "cook"), a woman I am pleased to call my real friend, is founder and president of Celebrate Kids, Inc. She is a champion at encouraging and equipping parents and educators to celebrate kids each and every day. According to Dr. Kathy, "parents and teachers who *celebrate kids* pay attention to children and teens for *who they are* and not just what they do, believe in kids' present value and not just their future potential, and encourage kids by celebrating them on more than their birthdays."

I first heard Dr. Kathy speak at our church on the topic "How Am I Smart?" I took my three kids (then in elementary school, junior high, and high school) to hear the presentation. Dr. Kathy affirmed her belief, based on solid research as well as on God's Word, that everyone has intelligence and talent. It's just that our schools and society tend to glorify and reward people who are "book smart" or "logic smart" or "music smart" but may not appreciate people who are "people smart" or "nature smart" or intelligent in other ways.[1] The impact her talk had on me and my youngest, Haley, can help you understand the importance of self-expression for your teen.

Haley is different from the rest of our family. She's the only athlete in a family of artists, dramatists, and musicians. She loves the outdoors; sometimes she must jump rope or she'll burst, and she has an amazing ability to read people. She is left-handed, and as a baby did most things backward before she did them forward; she even crawled backward.

When she got to be about five and learned to write, she wrote everything in mirror writing—backward and from right to left—even though what she was looking at was written left to right. She was wired in a unique way! Her kindergarten teacher explained that her brain had not developed fully and that within a year or two her writing would "flip," so it was nothing to worry about. (Personally I considered it an early sign of genius; didn't Leonardo DaVinci use mirror writing?) Her brain's unique wiring presented a challenge when she got around to adding and subtracting in columns. It's hard to keep the arithmetic straight when the numbers are flipped in your head.

Anyway, when Haley was in sixth grade, we heard Dr. Kathy's talk about "How Am I Smart?" It opened her eyes. Because she had to work harder to make words and figures line up in the right order, her confidence in her intelligence was shaken. Dr. Kathy affirmed Haley's visual giftedness—she has a real flair for color and fashion. She affirmed her love of the outdoors and athletics as being "nature smart" and "body smart" and her ability to read character as being "people smart." That affirmation has made a significant positive difference in Haley's self-perception.

I learned from Dr. Kathy—and knew from my decade of youth ministry—that every teen and young adult craves, needs, and longs for someone to pay attention to what they express of themselves through their unique talents and abilities. They long for affirmation, feedback, and even correction if it is done with love and a positive spin. Each person wants to be known and appreciated for his or her own unique personality and gifts. Especially in our media age where stars are larger than life, teens want to be noticed as special.

After Haley had been given some definitions to explain her unique gifts and affirm before the rest of us how she is smart, she felt encouraged. I think it helped her blossom. MySpace facilitates this kind of self-expression as nothing I've run across (and I've paid attention to this kind of thing for the ten years I was a youth pastor). Sure, you and I have heard the stories of girls putting up photos of themselves in just a bra and panties, or guys putting up photos that make them look like gangsters. Yes, the exhibitionistic teens are showing off in the wrong way with their racy photos, but this still shows how they are compelled to show off who they want themselves to be.

There are plenty of cases where teens are expressing themselves in positive, even beautiful or great ways on MySpace. But the news media doesn't highlight the beautiful photography Sarah (Haley's friend) creates or the many pieces of individual art being created and displayed on MySpace by teens. Some of the MySpace pages are works of digital art in themselves, requiring both skill and design talent to create. We would do well, and our teens would do better, if we focused our attention on those positive forms of self-expression. Teens will respond to whatever garners them attention; if they can't get attention for something good, they will aim to get attention for something bad. All the more reason for us as parents to pay attention to their positive self-expression on MySpace and affirm it; if we did, we would see a lot more that's positive.

So I want you to see how MySpace allows teens to express themselves and meet their needs for attention and affirmation. Let's start by having you experience how this works on MySpace on the most basic level, filling out the questions for your personal profile.

Experience It Online!

If you want to get the full experience, you can go to *www.myspace.com/ momsanddads* and check my blog for this chapter. There you can try out what I am describing here. If you want to go the noncomputer route, you can read what I have written in the remainder of the chapter.

Please take this seriously. Although you can have fun with it, it is important for the learning experience that you treat this exercise with respect. Also, plan to share what you write here with a few people who are close to you. Okay? This will be important down the line, so please don't skip it.

An Exercise in Self-Expression

Pick a quote you like or that characterizes you and write it here.

_____

_____

What are your interests?

_____

_____

_____

Who are your heroes?

_____

_____

_____

What are your favorite movies?

_____

_____

_____

What are your favorite TV shows?

_____

_____

_____

What are your favorite books?

_____

_____

_____

Who are your favorite musical artists?

_____

_____

_____

What are your favorite songs?

_____

_____

_____

What are your favorite musical styles?

_____

_____

_____

Of all the people who've ever lived or are living now, whom would you like to meet?

_____

_____

Describe yourself as if you were going to tell others about you.

_____

_____

_____

Who are your top eight friends?

_____

_____

_____

_____

If you could choose eight photos or snapshots to share with the people you care about, which would you choose? (If you have them handy, tuck them into this page of the book; if not, just describe them here from memory.) Write a caption for each one. Like: Look Mom, I Won the Trophy! or Family Christmas Photo 2005, or Thanksgiving at Yosemite with Friends).

Photo 1: _____

_____

Photo 2: _____

_____

Photo 3: _____

_____

Photo 4: _____

_____

Photo 5: _____

_____

Photo 6: _____

_____

Photo 7: _____

_____

Photo 8: _____

_____

What is your marital status? _____

_____

What is your religion? _____

_____

What is your education? _____

_____

How many children do you have? _____

_____

What is your occupation? _____

_____

If you could share your talents with the world, which would you choose: Music? Art? Photography? Drawing? Comedy? A scene from a play? A poem or piece of prose that captures your heart? A recipe you created? A photo of your trophy-winning sports team? The robot you built? The 1950s car you restored? Other?

_____

_____

Now, guess the answers *as you think your teen might answer them*: Pick a quote you like or that characterizes you and write it here.

_____

_____

What are your interests?

_____

_____

_____

Who are your heroes?

_____

_____

_____

What are your favorite movies?

_____

_____

_____

What are your favorite TV shows?

_____

_____

What are your favorite books?

_____

_____

_____

Who are your favorite musical artists?

_____

_____

_____

What are your favorite songs?

_____

_____

_____

What are your favorite musical styles?

_____

_____

_____

Of all the people who've ever lived or are living now, whom would you like to meet?

_____

_____

Describe yourself as if you were going to tell others about you.

_____

_____

_____

Who are your top eight friends?

_____

_____

_____

_____

If you could choose eight photos or snapshots to share with the people you care about, which would you choose? (If you have them handy, tuck them into this page of the book; if not, just describe them here from memory.) Write a caption for each one. Like: Look Mom, I Won the Trophy! or Family Christmas Photo 2005, or Thanksgiving at Yosemite with Friends):

Photo 1: _____

_____

Photo 2: _____

_____

Photo 3: _____

_____

Photo 4: _____

_____

Photo 5: _____

_____

Photo 6: _____

_____

Photo 7: _____

_____

Photo 8: _____

_____

What is your marital status? _____

_____

What is your religion? _____

_____

What is your education? _____

_____

How many children do you have? _____

_____

What is your occupation? _____

_____

If you could share your talents with the world, which would you choose: Music? Art? Photography? Drawing? Comedy? A scene from a play? A poem or piece of prose that captures your heart? A recipe you created? A photo of your trophy-winning sports team? The robot you built? The 1950s car you restored? Other?

_____

_____

▶ How Would You Feel?

Okay, if you put your heart into that, it probably took a while. Remembering that those pages have chronicled who you are as unique from anyone else, how would you react if I had authority over you and told you to take those pages and destroy them?

Record how you would feel here:

_____

_____

Maybe this exercise helps to explain what makes teenage guys weep when we tell them to "get off MySpace." It probably feels similar to what tearing out those pages would feel like for you. For the teens who have taken the time, care, and personal investment to write a profile, choose photos they like, recall music and movies they love, choose the color of the background and borders for the page, put in the code to create special design features, and share their heroes—that MySpace profile page is an expression of themselves. Deleting that is not deleting some*thing* online—something that doesn't matter—it feels more like deleting *me*.

Now let's look at the general forms of self-expression teens can use on MySpace.

The Basic Forms of Self-Expression Facilitated by MySpace

Here too I will connect unfamiliar buzz words and self-expression opportunities on MySpace to familiar ways of expressing oneself. The primary means of self-expression on MySpace can only be used by MySpace members. Let's compare these to things we know.

Familiar Form of Self-Expression	is like this	Form of Self-Expression on MySpace
Keeping a **private diary**		Keeping Blog set to Private.
Keeping a **journal** your friends can see and also share their thoughts with you		Keeping your Blog set to Friends Only.
Writing a column on topics of interest that is published		Writing a Blog set to Public.
Having your column syndicated and read regularly by people who like what you write		Keeping a Public Blog and having readers subscribe to your Blog (I subscribe to both my teens' blogs and have learned much and been impressed).
Writing a **travel log** and **giving a slide show** of travels (for your friends only or for public viewing)		Keeping a Blog about your travels with photos or a slide show included. (You can also add music that captures the theme of your travels.)

Familiar Form of Self-Expression	is like this	Form of Self-Expression on MySpace
Producing a "record album" without having to sell yourself to a record label		Posting your original Band Profile. Fans can communicate directly with you and copy one of your songs to their profile page to share with their friends.
Making a film that you show to your friends and others who are interested within your local reach		Making a Film and posting it on Filmmakers pages of MySpace for the whole world to see if they are interested in the subject or hear of it from "friends" via MySpace.
Making a **video**		Basically the same as above.
Creating a **comedy set or sketch** and **performing it for your local audience,** video taping it and copying it onto video tape or DVD		Creating a comedy set or sketch, performing it and recording it, then posting it on the Comedy section of MySpace.
An artist displaying her works of art in a gallery and inviting people to **come view her art,** mingling when they come.		Setting up an art gallery on your MySpace page where millions of people can view it and the artist can let anyone view her portfolio without having to print it. Guests mingle by using MySpace communication features. (Granted, there is a danger of losing control of your artwork.)
A photographer displaying her photography		Basically the same as above.

Artistic Self-Expression on MySpace

MySpace gives teens a place to showcase their talents and share their "artistry" with the world. Musicians can share their music in amazing ways! Even if Mom and Dad don't appreciate their particular taste in music, there's sure to be a group at MySpace music that understands and appreciates their genre of music. A budding musician gets quite a thrill to find out that people are hearing their music; it's more of a thrill to find fans taking that music and posting it on their profile pages so that one's musical gift goes around the world, spread by people who have listened to it and like it.

Those who sign up as musicians can post up to four of their musical pieces that people can hear, share, and comment on. It also automatically keeps a count of how many times each song has been played, downloaded, or shared. It even lets others download that song to their iPod so they can carry *your* music with them. Recently, MySpace has actually made a way for musicians to sell their music from the site.

Any artistic form—visual arts (which can be photographed and scanned or digitally transmitted), photography, comedy sketches (shared on audio files, video files, or podcasts), theatrical performances, film, animations, and all forms of writing—can be posted on MySpace in the form of films, videos, music, photographs, photo essays, and blogs.

Teens Are Writing Amazing Things!

Speaking of writing—since this is what I love to do and try to impart to others—have you noticed that teens are writing on MySpace? They are using MySpace to share essays, notes, letters, declarative positions, poetry, jokes, and all manner of written prose. Most parents would like to see their teens develop writing further.

Strange though it seems, teens seem to actually *enjoy* writing on MySpace. Why? I think it is because MySpace makes writing into what it was meant to be: a free flow of human-to-human communication. Because of the friend-to-friend origins of MySpace, the teens writing and creating there are uninhibited (granted, some are too uninhibited). Yes, there is plenty of drivel, but that's part of experimenting with self-expression. Amidst the drivel, there are gems of human expression.

If we would read what our teens are writing and affirm that which is good and real, they would blossom as writers. On MySpace they don't seem to worry about grammar, spelling, and punctuation or whether their participles are dangling. Nor do they worry that someone is going to come along and edit their posts with the dreaded red pen. As long as those reading the posts can understand the meaning, teen writers seem to be fine with that.

That's not to say that the free-wheeling nature of MySpace writing makes writing quality in general go down. One research study gave a home computer and internet access to low-income students who did not have a computer. After a year the students were tested; consistently their reading and writing skills improved remarkably. (Their math skills did not improve during the study.) This goes to show us that when teens are motivated to write and read, as they are on MySpace and other social networking sites, their skills in these areas improve—even though they are not paying attention to grammatical details in their online posts.

Generally speaking, teens love the freedom they have on MySpace to express themselves without being picked apart. They love being able to share their talents and know that people are hearing, seeing, or experiencing their art. They enjoy getting positive feedback, whether it's for a joke that only their small group "gets" and laughs at or for a piece of art or music appreciated by someone far away—Grandma, perhaps?

Ask Yourself

1. How has your teen expressed him or herself lately? How have you paid attention, celebrated their talents, affirmed their uniqueness?

Ask Your Teen

1. Ask your teen to tell you what he or she would *guess you would answer* for each of the questions above in the personal profile section.
2. Ask your teen to "check" what you guessed as his or her answers on the personal profile questions and tell you what you got right and what was way off.
3. Compare notes on how well or little you know each other, apart from knowing each other in your family roles.

Celebrate your teen! Find something unique and wonderful that you can affirm from what you learned in this exercise.

Make the MySpace Connection

If your teen has a personal profile, you don't have to guess at the answers to these questions. Ask if he or she would share some of it with you; then compare what you guessed to what they actually answered. It may take a few moments for your teen to make sure the profile is ready for Mom or Dad to see, but I would be surprised if any teen would not respond positively if they truly believe you are interested in getting to know and appreciate their unique form of self-expression.

If your teen doesn't have a MySpace personal profile page, ask if you can be shown one of their friend's pages. (I recommend that you have your teen choose, because they will naturally steer you away from vulgar or questionable material.) If you want to see my personal profile (different from my Moms and Dads MySpace page), that would be fine. It's at *www.myspace.com/conniewneal*.

Seeing a personal profile will let you see the basic form of self-expression. Reading the way people portray themselves and express themselves is fascinating. As I've checked out the personal profile pages of my best friends (some of whom I've known for over twenty-five years), I've been amazed at the things I learned about them that I did not know. I've also gotten to know my friends' teenage children as real people, and I've gotten to know the heart and artistry of many of my teens' friends.

In closing this chapter on how teens use MySpace for self-expression, let's do what Dr. Kathy Koch says we should do: pay attention to our teens for *who they are*, not just what they do. Let's believe in our teens' present value, not just their future potential. Encourage your teen by celebrating him or her today and celebrating their expressions of themselves. This will be good for you, better for your teen!

9

Going Places and Doing Things on MySpace

Would someone *really* plan their wedding through MySpace? Apparently so; this is not so surprising in this age of e-planning almost anything. When I started checking to see what kinds of events people were actually planning within five hundred miles of my home, I found over 340 weddings, 80 graduations, 260 reunions, over 60 Sweet Sixteen parties, over 80 baby showers, 40 charity events, 80 fundraisers, and one baptism.

My son, Taylor, was thrilled to be asked to open for a well-known concert artist in our area, but he didn't get much time to promote the event. So he planned his concert as an event on MySpace. That meant that all 356 of his "fans" and friends were notified immediately of the event, asked to RSVP, sent a flier, and offered a reminder. We were pleased to see that this approach to event planning worked so well that those who reported they were there to see Taylor exceeded those who said they came for the main performer!

A big part of teenage social life revolves around going places and doing things. "What's happening?" is more than a catchphrase; it's a vital question teens need an answer to so they can be wherever "it" is happening. MySpace has a useful feature that facilitates planning and announcing events, inviting friends, getting those invited to give you an immediate RSVP, keeping a running count of how many guests are planning to attend, and even offering to put the event on the guest's MySpace calendar and to remind them of the event in advance. How cool is that?

Here's a list of some of the things the "Events" feature can do on MySpace:

- Invite select friends to your personal event, or everyone on your MySpace "friends" list.

- Get immediate RSVP reply and ongoing count of how many plan to attend.
- Send or pass along an online flier promoting a public event with contact information.
- Offer links to find directions to the event.
- Offer links to purchase tickets to public events right on the "Event flier" page.
- Browse events happening in your area and areas of interest; get immediate information.
- Promote your events without spending any money.
- Let people "test out" the entertainment at an event before deciding to go (for example, have link to music of a concert artist accompany the invitation or have a link to the band's profile page).
- Use MySpace calendar to keep track of events you want to attend.
- Others who say yes to your event invitation can have that automatically added to their MySpace calendar, with optional reminder sent so as not to forget to attend.

If someone is planning an event, especially a public event like a graduation, MySpace "Events" can make sending invitations a breeze. You simply fill out a form and click "Invite Friends" and all your "friends" receive the invitation. This is another reason teens must be diligent about keeping their friends limited only to the people they'd like to have arrive at their event. The form covers the basics. You simply click "Events" on the menu bar across the top of the MySpace home page and follow the directions. Careful thought should be given before using this feature for private events. Even though you limit your guest list, the recipients can pass it on to anyone with a click.

Filling Out the Form for an Event

The form to create an event looks something like this:

MySpace offers a guide to help those using the "Events" function to think through the implications of their decisions.

MySpace Events

Events Links

Event Invites

Events I've Posted

Events I'm Attending

Create New Event

MySpace Events   Events Home | Create Event | My Calendar

Create An Event   Invite Friends

What's Going On?	When?
Event Name: *	Start Date:
	December ▾ 5 ▾ 2006 ▾
Event Organizer: *	Start Time:
Connie Neal	7 ▾ : 00 ▾ PM ▾
Contact E-mail: (huh?)	Where:?
cwneal@surewest.net	
Event Type: (huh?) Category *	Place/Venue:
◉ Public ▾	
○ Private	Address:
Age Limit:	
◉ All Ages ○ 18 and Over ○ 21 and Over	City
Short Description (no HTML):	
	State Postal Code Country
	Alabama ▾ United States ▾
Long Description (HTML OK):	
	[Save Event]

* Required fields

Public or Private?

Events listed on MySpace can be either "public" (viewable by anyone) or "private" (viewable by invitation only). It's totally up to you, and you can switch your event any time.

Public events: If you make your event public, it will show up on the MySpace Events page (under the category you choose), and any MySpace user or visitor can check it out and possibly attend. You can still invite individual friends, both on and off MySpace, and you can even have an RSVP so you know who's coming.

Private events: If you only want the people you invite to see your event page, make it private. This is usually the best option for events like birthday parties, TV nights, and so on, where you only want people you know to come to your event.

Show the Guest List to Everyone

Your "Event" page can display the names and pictures of the people you've invited.

If you want all invitees to be able to see the guest list, leave the box **checked**.

If you want to be the only one who can see the guest list, **uncheck** the box.

Ask Invitees to RSVP on Event Page

Your event page can show who's coming, who might be attending, who can't make it, and who hasn't responded yet.

If you want invitees to RSVP on your event page, leave the box **checked**.

If you *don't* want invitees to be able to RSVP, **uncheck** the box.

Allow Comments

MySpace users can leave comments on your "Event" page, just as they can do on profiles. You can control who can leave comments.

"Anyone" lets any invitee or visitor (public) leave comments.

"Only Attendees" lets users who have RSVP'd that they're attending or might be attending to comment.

"No One" disables commenting on your event page.

Contact Email

Optional. If you list a contact email. it will display as a link on the "Event" page.

If you don't want a contact email displayed, just leave the field blank. MySpace users can still contact you by going to your profile at *http://events.MySpace.com* (Events).

Before I even knew the "Events" feature existed, I experienced it! I received an email in my primary email account—not MySpace— telling me that Taylor was inviting me to an event. I clicked on the link and was taken to a flier of Taylor's upcoming concert at a local coffee-house. This was now a MySpace page. It asked if I planned to attend. I clicked yes and it asked me how many guests.

Next a message appeared offering to put this on my MySpace cal-endar. I didn't even know I had a MySpace calendar! Sure, I said, now curious. It took me to a calendar page for the date of the concert and there was the event, already logged in for me. Then I was asked if I would like to be reminded by email and how many days in advance. I said yes, and selected two days in advance. It took a moment or two, click, click, click, and I was back at work.

Two days before the event I received an email reminder. By clicking on the link in that reminder I was again taken to the flier with all the information I needed. Just the time I saved—much of which may have been spent searching my house for lost fliers and looking for directions—makes this feature appealing to me!

Managing Risks While Using MySpace Events Functions

The "Events" feature is one point on MySpace where virtual reality meets reality. Whenever a date, time, and location are given, one has to take precautions to make sure that unwanted "guests" don't show up to make trouble. Teens may be so taken by how convenient the "Events" feature is that they do not take precautions to make sure that this feature doesn't turn their event into a real-life danger zone. Therefore, we as parents should be careful to monitor our teen's use of this feature. Parents can do the following:

1. Limit the "Events" feature to invitations to public events. Risks are significantly reduced if this feature is only used for public events.
2. Check over the "friends" list carefully before your teen sends out an invitation. Delete anyone who is questionable *before* sending the invitation.
3. Offer to coordinate the event invitations for the teen.

10

Engaging the Wider World:
Forums and Chat Rooms on MySpace

In 2002, fifteen-year-old Katie Canton met twenty-two-year-old John (last name withheld) in a live, online chat room. Since he lived on the other side of the country, Katie felt free to flirt and send photos by email. Soon John was sending Katie gifts, phone cards for long conversations, and numerous emails. "John told me, 'Age is just a number; love can be anywhere with anyone,'" Katie recalls. "He even told me he wanted to marry me, and I believed him. If my parents had tried to separate us at that point, it only would have added to the drama that made it exciting. I thought I was in love."

When John planned to fly cross-country to visit Katie in San Francisco, her parents consulted a friend in the local police department. By this point, there was no way to "talk sense" into Katie. So this friend gave the family a video game created by Web Wise Kids (*www.wired withwisdom.org*) entitled *Missing*. Katie's parents insisted she play the game that lets teens virtually experience tracking an online sex predator. Katie reluctantly saw for herself that her relationship with John fit a pattern well known by law enforcement personnel.

Katie turned over all the gifts, emails, letters, and computer files she'd exchanged with John, and the San Francisco Police Department discovered he was the primary suspect in the rape of a thirteen-year-old girl who'd also met him in a chat room. Katie finally met John when she testified at his trial where he was convicted and sent to prison for twenty years. Katie credits what she learned from *Missing* with sparing her more harm than she'd already experienced. She now encourages kids to be savvy online surfers as an ambassador to youth for Web Wise Kids. Her parents learned how dangerous online forums and chat rooms can be (anywhere, of course, but this includes on MySpace).[1]

I can learn a lot about my teens from checking out the groups to which they belong (and so can anyone else if the profile is not set to private). As one of your preliminary conditions for allowing your teen to have a MySpace page, I recommend that you be allowed to be a "friend" if you promise not to invade his or her "space" in any way that draws attention to yourself. Here's what Taylor listed on his profile page about his groups:

Groups:	this holiday life fans, Natomas Charter, Charter Pride 07, Euphoric (U4IC), Remembering Brian, Red-Heads Unite, NCS Drama Department, BLAKE ATTACK!
	View All Taylor's Groups

When I click on "View All Taylor's Groups," I see thumbnails and names of the groups to which he belongs. Since he has either created these groups or chosen to belong to them, they tell me a lot about him and where he sees himself fitting into the world and who wants him. I can then click on any of these groups and be taken to that group's page. It tells me: Category, date founded, location, how many members, name of the group leader, and a button to click to join (if it's a public group).

Even if it's not a private group, think twice about joining your teen's group, as you may discover where you belong and where you *don't* belong if you are told you are not wanted in that group. Remember, teens *do need their space*!

Within the group there are forum topics exclusive to that group, the ability to post bulletins just to that group, and the ability to see all the group members. A forum set up for a group with a good purpose and members serving a good purpose will not be in the same range of danger as a forum for a general group. In fact, this can be a positive way to communicate on a shared topic. Some youth pastors use MySpace or other social networking group forums to carry on small group discussions after the weekly Bible study. So please don't assume that all forums are bad.

Expanding Circle of MySpace "Friends" to "Friends" of "Friends"

One aspect of MySpace considered cool, and certainly interesting, is that you can go from your profile page, to the pages of your "friends" (whom you may or may not know in real life), to the profile pages of those people listed as "friends" of your friends on their MySpace profile page. All the people who are friends of the friends of your friends are said to be in your extended network. I have twenty-one "friends" on my MySpace profile page, but my extended network includes 123,892,899 pages of a friend of a friend of a friend.

This feature is a good way for real friends to introduce people they think will enjoy each other's company. It is also interesting to see whom a person associates with and the kind of people they hang out with. But this is also where your teen is far more likely to encounter offensive material, because when we get a few circles out beyond our chosen circle of friends, we may likely find ourselves in a whole different culture.

But please remember: if your teen's profile is set to private, only their friends can view it, not their extended network. That's a big step toward keeping them safe until they can demonstrate the good sense needed to manage more independence. If someone in your teen's extended network has a profile set to private, your teen will only be able to see the default photo, headline quote, and basic information.

Risk Management for Friends of Friends

There are many ways your teen can manage the risks involved here. Make sure they are aware of these tips:

1. Don't venture to meet friends of friends.
2. Set profile to private so that the extended network cannot look in on you.
3. The default photo and quote tell you something about how the person represents him or herself; use discretion. If the friend of a friend's picture doesn't look like someone you'd invite into your home, think twice before clicking on it.
4. Don't assume that because someone is a friend of a friend they are safe.

Remember, if you don't know the person in person before meeting them on MySpace, you don't know who they are. *SK8R Boy 15* could be that fat, socially maladapted, middle-aged guy from the *Saturday Night Live* sketch. Therefore, don't give out personal information or agree to meet someone in person just on the basis of his being a MySpace "friend" of one of your MySpace "friends."

Venturing into Forums or Chat Rooms

In my opinion, forums pose the greatest risk for MySpace users. So pay close attention to this section. However, as I've talked to teens (a very informal survey), they tell me most of them don't use the forums very much, if at all. While this kind of survey is unscientific, it may be all you need if you make your own survey of your teen and his friends. Ask your teen and their friends if they have found any MySpace forums that they like. Ask if it is a "public" forum or a "private" forum. If it's a private forum made up of students from their chemistry class working collaboratively on homework, that's light years away from a public forum they stumbled across on MySpace on a questionable topic.

A forum on MySpace is an ongoing discussion—a public forum—in real time where previous discussion posts are archived so people can go in and join the discussion and go back through previous posts to see what people said on the topic. People participating in the forums are free to say whatever they want to say. Profanity is not censored and is commonplace. If someone in a forum violates the prohibition against hate speech or harassment (commonly known as flaming), the forum participants or moderator can block that person from that forum, but not every forum has a moderator.

One should not venture into a forum expecting that they will be protected from reading mean comments or the F*** word. It's an open, public environment, frequented by older users, and open to what most parents would consider offensive. Sadly, teens have told me that they are so used to hearing such language in everyday life, especially at school, that they just learn to block it out.

A chat room is the specific location or page where each forum discussion topic is being discussed. Chat rooms create a far greater risk than just communicating with people your teen knows. Sexual predators have found chat rooms to be a prime opportunity to seek out easy prey. If they can get into a private conversation with someone who has been chatting with the group—which can be done by switching to email or instant messaging—the predator can zero in on that person or take note of her and follow up by trying to check out her profile or sending a friend request.

If your teen uses a real photo of himself as the default photo, everyone in the chat room in the forum discussion can see it. Nowadays police posing as bait also go to chat rooms, often to attract sexual predators. MySpace has gotten press for the dangers, but less so for the times law enforcement have used it to catch the predators.

The forums on MySpace include a wide array of general topics, with an even wider array of discussion threads taking place. Here is a list of the general topics for forums:

Health & Fitness Work it in here; exchange tips, find a gym buddy.	Chat	24073	354108	Mon Dec 4, 2006 1:24 PM by: **Steve** » **View Post**
Love & Relationships Everyone's favorite topics, of course.	Chat	51945	1775052	Mon Dec 4, 2006 1:26 PM by: **nosson** » **View Post**
Movies Film buffs can buff here. Movie Reviews perhaps?	Chat	3996	105628	Mon Dec 4, 2006 1:25 PM by: **Christina** » **View Post**
Music Indie, mainstream and whatever suits your fancy.	Chat	365030	4396145	Mon Dec 4, 2006 1:26 PM by: **Earl 2.0** » **View Post**
MySpace Topics related to MySpace--users, help, & general nonsense.	Chat	387029	1168605	Mon Dec 4, 2006 1:26 PM by: **Mrs Peaches** » **View Post**
News & Politics War is mean politics.	Chat	79839	1840755	Mon Dec 4, 2006 1:26 PM by: **Chris (L-FL)** » **View Post**
Religion & Philosophy Let's be nice. Remember what Socrates said.	Chat	38721	1625565	Mon Dec 4, 2006 1:25 PM by: **Tommy Flavell (solo)** » **View Post**
Science It's rumored that Carl Sagan actually created MySpace.	Chat	5871	75896	Mon Dec 4, 2006 1:19 PM by: **miss anthrope** » **View Post**
Sports You got game b-baller?	Chat	28507	473190	Mon Dec 4, 2006 1:26 PM by: **[ekk] t-nasty [ekk]** » **View Post**
Television There is more to TV than the OC.	Chat	18570	325861	Mon Dec 4, 2006 1:22 PM by: **Liz** » **View Post**
Travel & Vacations Get the latest getaways and travel deals.	Chat	11075	38155	Mon Dec 4, 2006 1:00 PM by: **maggie** » **View Post**

The user picks a general forum category or folder and clicks on it, and subcategories appear. As with most things in life, it's the choices our teens make that determine the kind of experience they will have further down the line of that forum category. Let's take two possible paths to see the wide divergence of possibilities based on what we choose:

Forum Home » Religion & Philosophy

Forum Sub Category	Topics	Posts
General	5616	157352
Philosophy	7160	179065
Religion	25948	1289173

Suppose I want to see what's being discussed about Christianity. I choose the Religion folder. If I click on the religion folder, a list of 1 – 15 specific discussion threads are listed out of a total of 22,144. I clicked on the topic Jesus — about as safe a topic as I thought I'd find — and found a mix of sanctity and sacrilege. Even here I found the F*** word, but, ironically, from someone who was trying to stop people from putting down another person's faith. Here's a sampling of what I found on that day (grammar and punctuation are those of the writers):

Salina: I ♥ God. Are there any other Christians?

Greiner: You want to be just like Jesus? A man? Who doesn't have sex? Who doesn't respect His mother?

Slayer: You want to be a myth?

Father John: You people can be so cruel.

Corey   (Responding to a previous thread) ... but Jesus never had laser eyes!

Adam: You guys are not funny so F*** OFF. Trampling on the beliefs of others is moronic.

Black Eden: You just said God's name in vain ... wait, that's a heart? I heart God? Sorry sweetie, but your heart is an emotionless organ ;D

Greiner wrote: (quoting Corey, and responding to) ... but Jesus never had laser eyes!
                 Maybe on the 2nd coming ... Jesus 2.0...

DNAunion: Wouldn't that be Jesus 3.0? I thought the Mormons saw Jesus here in the New World, hundreds of years after He died in Jerusalem.

There were a few more comments that I found too offensive to even relate with ***s blocking out some of the letters. One was a reference to Jesus being Jewish, but I wasn't sure if that was meant to be a racial slur or not. An open forum is an *open* forum. You cannot control who is in the "room" and their power to speak/write, nor can moderators get ahead of the live action to curb any inappropriate content instantly. If your teen is going into a chat room to take part in a forum, it is far more challenging than communicating with friends, and more precautions must be taken.

You may want to classify general forums in another level of danger and prohibit their use entirely until your teen is older and has demonstrated maturity. Then you may want to venture into forums together at first for mentoring purposes.

Risk Management in Forums

Be sure your teen is aware of the basic, commonsense safety tips for forum use.

1. Expect there to be at least one offensive person in the room. Prepare to handle that kind of intellectual assault.
2. Have a default photo that is generic rather than specific to you—and certainly not sexually provocative.
3. Have your profile set to private or friends only so people who "meet" you or argue with you in the forum can't see your profile.
4. Don't go into forum topics that are likely to go in the direction of sexual discussions or other topics that could lead to danger areas for you.
5. Don't reply to an IM from anyone who IMs you from the chat room. More cautious yet, have your settings adjusted to not receive IMs while you're in a forum.
6. Be nice; no matter how offensive someone is to you, responding in the same vein only escalates the friction.

MySpace Precautions to Protect Younger Users in Forums

A brochure I received states the following:

MySpace restricts inappropriate content from being visible to specific age groups. Some MySpace "groups" that engage in adult discussions are inappropriate for minors and have been reported to the MySpace staff as such. These groups are designated as "adult only" and are blocked from being listed on the Groups List available on MySpace. Non-registrants (individuals without MySpace accounts attempting to utilize MySpace.com) and registered users under 18 are unable to access or join adult-only groups. The adult-only groups also incorporate a click-through warning for users under 18 that attempt to view the group.[2]

This is helpful as far as it goes. Since MySpace has no way to verify the age of its users, anyone can say they are any age. Thus, underage users intent on getting into adult discussions can do so by lying about their age. However, with these safety precautions in place, your teen will never stumble into an adult group or forum by accident.

Forums Can Create Positive Conversations Too

Now let's look at the second pathway a forum can take. Forums can be a positive way for people with similar tastes or interests to converse. Here's an example of a place where music lovers would be likely to find some positive conversations. In Music Forums I found the following categories:

Forum Home » Music

Forum Sub Category	Topics	Posts
Acoustic	11849	94248
Alternative	18971	131825
Electronic/Dance	20190	182333
Emo	20031	368871
General	88701	958077
Hardcore	13336	134451
Hip-Hop	88669	929078
Metal	32322	554236
Punk	25961	367845
Rock	45010	675263

Just as we would probably not go to a concert featuring some of these kinds of music, we can judge from the genre of music that we would or would not want to venture into some of these forums and would enjoy others. Just as certain types of concerts tend to draw a certain type of crowd, so too as the MySpace users choose the topic, to a large degree they are choosing the group. Common sense and a little knowledge of the category should enable someone to make a pretty good guess of what the atmosphere in the chat rooms for that forum might be.

In general, forums are on the far end of the independence scale. For the moment, I'm happy that my teens aren't interested, but if your teen is, this area requires close monitoring. If you know what forums your teen has been to, you can go in later and read the transcripts of the discussions. Public forums can work to a parent's advantage too.

Classifieds

Another group type of function on MySpace is the "Classifieds." Classifieds on MySpace are pretty much like classifieds anywhere, with two huge differences that impact your teen's safety and well-being. The people posting the classifieds are not necessarily who they present themselves to be. The ads can lead to another site off of MySpace that may be dangerous to your teen in any number of ways and possibly dangerous to your computer as well, since MySpace cannot monitor links to third-party sites. A red flag should go up in your mind and your teen's mind before clicking on any hyperlink from a classified to a third-party site.

We as parents must be especially careful whenever our teens engage the real world on the internet, whether that is through MySpace or any other social networking site. However, there are also positive ways teens can use MySpace to fulfill their basic developmental needs. We turn our attention to that in the next chapter.

Using MySpace to Fulfill
Five Developmental Needs

Teens are in the process of figuring out their core needs and developing their *individual* identity apart from their identity as your child. Teens have to figure out who they are apart from their parents if they are to grow up to be healthy adults.

When teens navigate MySpace, they are also navigating the important developmental milestones of adolescence. I'm not saying that they are conscious of working on filling these needs; it's just human nature to do so, and MySpace may facilitate this quest without their even realizing it.

To accomplish these essential developmental tasks teens do *need* some private space (which is *not* to say unsupervised). There are many ways teens get the "space" they need: they may retreat to their room alone, or go for a walk, or write in a diary, or they may use MySpace to help them in many of these tasks. Let's look at how teens *might* use MySpace to get them from where they are to where we want them to be, to becoming fulfilled adults who contribute something of value to the world.

My friend Dr. Kathy Koch again has helped me understand this. In her book[1] and DVD[2] Dr. Kathy explains the five core needs we all have. In order to mature, we must answer five questions about ourselves (see figure on page 117).

The primary need that forms the foundation or basis for all the others is security. That's where we parents have almost solely focused our attention when it comes to our teens and MySpace. However, our teens are rightfully and necessarily focused on all five areas. I will show you in this chapter how teens can use MySpace to facilitate developing in all of these areas. As I explain what is going on in your teen's heart and mind developmentally in the context of these core needs, I will show

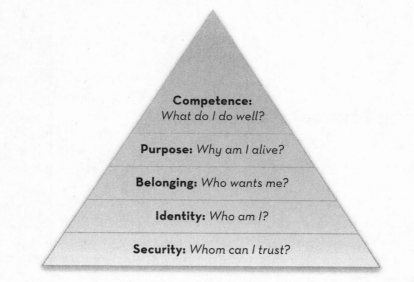

Competence:
What do I do well?

Purpose: *Why am I alive?*

Belonging: *Who wants me?*

Identity: *Who am I?*

Security: *Whom can I trust?*

you the MySpace functions that they may or may not be using in each area. By doing this I hope you will be able to see ways that teens might use MySpace to go from telling you, "I need my space!" to finding their place in the larger world.

We do need to address security issues, which we will look at more closely in the chapters on safety. But if we focus solely on security, we will miss the big picture. As you read through this chapter, zoom out enough to refocus on all your teen's core needs and how he or she may be developing in these areas within the context of MySpace. If your teen is not on a social networking site, think through how each of these core needs are being met and how each of the related self-asked questions are being answered in his or her life.

Security: Whom Can I Trust?

The need for security is essential for every person at every age. Teens are asking themselves *Whom can I trust?* in their interpersonal relationships—with regard to their parents, government, school officials, friends, and even religious communities. However, when it comes to the internet, it seems that parents are much more worried about security than are their teens. Teens seem to think that they are taking enough security precautions, but confirming that can help put parent's worries to rest.

Identity: Who Am I?

The need to figure out one's identity is a key part of adolescence for all teens. They have to get to know themselves as individuals within their family of origin, but also within their peer groups and within the world. The search for identity has a lot to do with a teen's inclination to go through changes in hairstyles, fashion, interest, and even groups with which he or she associates. Teens must work out their identity before they can individuate successfully to become well-adjusted adults. Their ability to build a healthy and realistic identity is dependent on feeling secure enough to step out to discover who they are.

Belonging: Who Wants Me?

The need to belong, to be accepted, to fit in, is huge during adolescence (which is why parents rightfully worry about peer pressure). On MySpace belonging comes into play in terms of who is on your teen's "friends" list, whose "friends" list your teen is on, and which groups they are affiliated with. On MySpace, users can join groups or create groups to which they belong. If they put down the name of their school when filling out their profile, they will automatically be added to the group of students at their school.

The question "Who wants me?" brings up the subject of how teens use MySpace to pursue romantic interests, crushes, and all the drama that makes up high school life for many teens. Here are some ways:

- Sharing photos can be a way of flirting.
- They can browse or be "browsed" by others.
- They can pass notes, set up dates, and get to know people they are interested in.
- They can be approached by those interested in them for romantic or sexual reasons.
- They can display their sense of modesty or lack thereof.
- They can display and see displayed by their "friends" their sense of morality, amorality, or immorality in interpersonal romantic relationship.

How our teens manage being wanted by others and presenting themselves to the opposite sex can tell you a lot about how they see themselves. If you notice something of concern on your teen's page and

MySpace presence, you need to do more than just have them delete that page. You need to address the core needs and any problems that have surfaced. There are some books listed on pages 211–213 that may prove helpful in this area.

The question of belonging also applies to the family. Teens in past generations generally met their need to know where they belonged within their extended family, usually located within a small radius. In the past few generations, however, the ability to travel easily and the soaring divorce rate has combined to pretty much destroy the extended family network for many teens. MySpace provides a way for teens who are interested to meet people in their extended family and share information and photos. This can supply a need for belonging that can benefit our teens. With MySpace, teens can reconnect and stay connected to far-flung family members no matter where they live. Think of the power in that.

Purpose: Why Am I Alive?

Everybody wants to have a purpose; if teens are confident that they can make positive contributions, they will be less likely to make negative ones. MySpace can help in this regard. Since MySpace has become the most popular social networking site and a known gathering place for teens, many groups promoting social issues, political causes, branches of the military, and religious organizations have turned to MySpace to reach recruits for their causes or to spread their message. A teen looking to discover why she is alive can find many good causes to participate with to make a positive difference in the world.

Let me give you one example. Invisible Children is an organization promoting social action primarily on the part of teens through showing the film *Invisible Children*, which exposes the terrible plight of children in war-torn Uganda. The film has been shown at high schools across the country and has sought to raise awareness and funds to provide healthcare, safety, employment, and education for Ugandan children. Teens see the film and are touched. But with MySpace they can *do* something. There are now over sixty separate MySpace pages promoting the Invisible Children mission.

The "official" Invisible Children MySpace page has this quote from a teacher:

Invisible Children has changed our school and the lives of our students forever. I cannot put into words what it means to be a teacher and watch my students, some of which seemed apathetic to everything, become completely and utterly dedicated to helping kids that they will most likely never meet. The ultimate goal for me as a teacher is to create circumstances that allow kids to realize that they are part of a bigger world and that they hold the knowledge, resources, and power to be a voice for those who have none. IC has created an outlet of caring, hope, and active involvement for my students, provided a way for my kids to be a member of a global community, and helped them to believe that they can make a difference.

—Connie Ring, teacher, Mueller High School[3]

In pages like these and many more, teens are *wanted* and told that their lives have *purpose*, and they are given a way to make a positive difference by making donations, attending fundraising concerts, spreading the message, and forming groups to help a cause—whatever that cause may be—in various ways.

Imagine how empowering that kind of connectedness to the needs of others might be for teens looking to find their purpose, to make a difference in the world, and to discover their competencies. Teens are getting used to using the tremendous power of the internet. If they get connected to social action causes, that power can be harnessed for tremendous good.

Competence: What Do I Do Well?

Any teen who has seen *Napoleon Dynamite* knows competence is all about having skills. To quote Napoleon, "You know, like nunchuck skills, bow-hunting skills, computer-hacking skills ... girls only want boyfriends who have great skills." Teens can gain many skills by what they learn on MySpace.

The pinnacle of fulfillment of our human needs—and our teen's developmental needs during adolescence—is *competence*, finding the answer to the question *What do I do well?* Gaining the skills associated with proficient, safe, and responsible MySpace use or social networking develops competence in itself. Teens who are avid social networkers become more confident in their abilities to communicate effectively, express themselves in various ways, read and write better, and hone interpersonal skills.

But the possibilities go further than that. As teens learn to design their MySpace page, they are developing computer skills. They may be motivated to learn specific computer programs, such as Flash Animation, because they want to "trick out" their MySpace page and think that will help.

They can also go further and gain competence by what they do *through* MySpace. If they are making good choices about the groups they associate with and the social issues they discover, our teens can connect with great causes to make a difference in the world. They can learn and grow and participate in events that help them discover what they do well. If they are expressing themselves on MySpace and getting comments, that feedback can help them figure out what they do well. When our teens use technology and social networking, they are developing competencies that will serve them well in future jobs, educational situations, and life in general.

Fulfilling the Five Needs

Finding ways to fulfill these five needs isn't a neat, easy path. It's a messy, complicated journey, filled with detours and setbacks, joyous discoveries and soul-crushing disappointments. Your job as a parent is not to make your teen's journey for her but to monitor her progress and, in general, to keep her pointed toward positive ways that she can fulfill her needs.

This positive progress toward the fulfillment of your teen's core needs isn't automatic; moving in the direction of what is right always takes more effort than going toward what is easy. For possible good to overcome the gravitational slide toward evil—on MySpace and in life—effort and determination are required. When people point out that much of what is found on MySpace flows downward in terms of its moral value, they have a valid point. However, that isn't the way it has to be.

If people *choose* to use MySpace for good, it has the power to facilitate good in every area of core human needs. But all that is necessary for evil to triumph—on MySpace or anywhere—is for good people to do nothing. If we determine to use social networking for good and guide our teens along the way, good can triumph.

To help you monitor your child's progress in the five core areas, carefully and thoughtfully answer the questions below.

How Is Your Teen Working Toward Fulfilling the Five Core Needs?

If your teen already has a MySpace page, you may wish to look at it with these questions in mind. If they do not have a MySpace page, think about how they are developing in each of the five areas of core needs. Then write your observations below. Your answers to the following questions could determine whether you allow them to use MySpace, and if so, at what level you can trust them to use it. Once you determine that, you will be better able to protect your child using the tips in chapters 14 through 16.

Ask Yourself

1. Look to see how well your teen manages *security*. Is he aware of who can and cannot be trusted?

   _____

   _____

   _____

2. Look to see how your teen perceives her *identity*. How does she define herself on her MySpace profile page? If she doesn't yet use MySpace, how do her friends, interests, activities, tastes, and clothing reflect her identity?

   _____

   _____

   _____

   _____

3. Look to see where your teen thinks he *belongs*. Who wants him? Where does he see himself fitting in?

_____

_____

_____

_____

4. Look to see what your teen thinks her *purpose* is for being alive. What causes or needs excite her? Where does she want to make a difference?

_____

_____

_____

_____

5. Look to see how your teen perceives his *competence*. What does your teen think he does well?

_____

_____

_____

_____

Part 4

Parental Decisions about MySpace

12

Growing Your Teen's Independence Using MySpace

The teenage years are all about growing in independence (and inter-dependence with a circle larger than one's immediate family). Social networking offers teens several ways they can facilitate growing inde-pendence. They can consider various beliefs, listen or join in on forums, investigate ideas, flirt, go places, and do things. All these developmen-tal pursuits are facilitated by MySpace.

They can also meet new people and get involved in any aspect of life that catches their interest by meeting others who share that interest. I know — this is a scary thought! They can get into trouble if they take in disturbing ideas or mingle with people who are a bad influence. This can also be a danger zone if teens venture to exert their independence in socially unacceptable, rebellious, or dangerous ways, but they can also use MySpace positively as they grow in independence.

Parenting: A Journey toward Our Child's Independence as an Adult

Parenting is a journey that starts with our children being totally depen-dent on us. Our goal is to help them grow, step by step, toward becom-ing responsibly independent. As we do so, we must prepare them to make good choices and help them stay safe at each step along the way.

If we will think back to this life progression when we were the teens taking the steps toward independence, we'll remember a differ-ent perspective. We didn't think in terms of the dangers; we thought in terms of the rewards, the freedom. The stair steps of adolescence toward independence include both greater risks and dangers along with greater rewards and freedom. The trick is to manage the steps safely and responsibly.

127

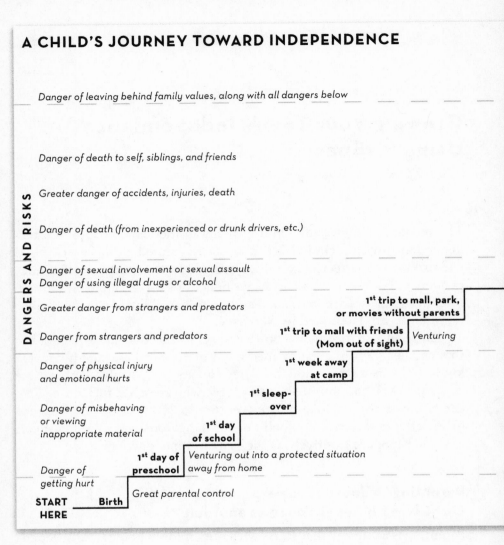

A CHILD'S JOURNEY TOWARD INDEPENDENCE

Baby Steps toward Independence

I vividly remember the first day of school for each of my children. I remember what clothes they wore, where we took the first-day-of-school photo, and how each one looked going through the door. I bet you remember that for your children too. There's something about letting them out of our control, seeing them take that step away from us and toward a lifetime of growing independence that grabs our attention and emblazons the memory in our mind.

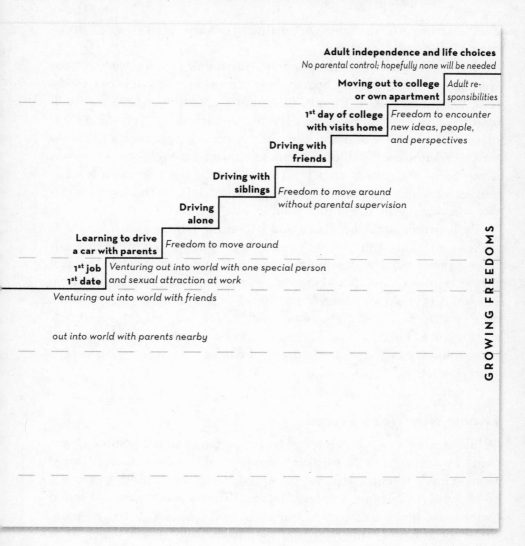

Adult independence and life choices
No parental control; hopefully none will be needed

Moving out to college | *Adult re-*
or own apartment | *sponsibilities*

1st day of college | *Freedom to encounter*
with visits home | *new ideas, people,*
and perspectives

Driving with
friends

Driving with
siblings | *Freedom to move around*
without parental supervision

Driving
alone

Learning to drive
a car with parents | *Freedom to move around*

1st job | *Venturing out into world with one special person*
1st date | *and sexual attraction at work*

Venturing out into world with friends

out into world with parents nearby

GROWING FREEDOMS

Parents who homeschool don't have that first-day-of-school experience, but we all took note of the first sleepover, the first week away at camp, the first trip to the mall or park with friends (with Mom or Dad keeping an eye on their group without being noticed), the first trip to the movie theater without a parent, and so on. We certainly noticed the first date, the first time they drove the car, the first time they drove a car without us with them. If we have children old enough, we felt a certain pang at their first day of college, even if they came home on visits. Their first day moving away from our home—whether to their own apartment or to college or getting married—marked a milestone in our lives as well as theirs.

This same pattern corresponds to our teen's progressive steps toward independence on MySpace: their ventures into a circle of friends, to a widening circle of friends, to groups and forums where they will hear ideas or see things perhaps foreign to our values, to finding their place in the larger world and hopefully making a positive contribution for the greater good. All of that can take place on MySpace. However, if our teens are getting ahead of themselves by leaping into a level of danger for which they are not prepared or into forums that are destructive, they are going to get into trouble.

By learning about MySpace and becoming familiar with how it is used by our teens and how it fits into their lives, we can make sure our teen is prepared to stay safe while growing in independence. You still may end up deciding that MySpace isn't right for your teen at this time. However, if you understand the various levels of danger, you can make sure your teen is growing savvy enough to stay safe on any social networking site. This is advised because social networking is quickly gaining popularity as the primary means of communication among today's teen generation.

I Know Why We're Scared

While at a meeting for parents of teens learning about MySpace (I was there as a parent, not a speaker), the tone of the conversation varied from scared, to confused, to concerned, to overwhelmed, to scared, to hopeful, to curious, to scared again. Whatever our parental mood swings, our heads told us that our teens will have access to MySpace, other social networking sites, and the internet whether it scares us or not.

Scott, one of the fathers there, said it well: "Most of us have kids who have played organized sports. And our kids have probably been injured, whether their feelings are hurt by being cut from the lineup or they've been injured physically. We know that's part of youth, that's part of growing up. We've been there ourselves. Most of us have played youth sports and we've gotten hurt and we've lived. I know why this is so scary for us; with MySpace we've never been there. We don't know what it is; we didn't grow up with all these options or the technology. So we don't have our own experience to draw from to reassure ourselves that even though there are dangers, our kids will be okay. Personally, my kids have gotten hurt a lot more playing sports than on the internet."

Scott's comments seemed to calm the group—a nervous calm, but calm nonetheless. However, we must also bear in mind that because we don't know and haven't experienced MySpace for ourselves, we really don't know how dangerous it is. We may worry that it might be *more* dangerous than we think. So how are we to handle this?

I think the best way to handle our teen's growing independence on MySpace is to see it as a series of graduated stair steps similar to the ones in real life. There are levels of risk and safety skills that can be learned to manage that risk progressively. The lessons we've learned as we've helped our teens manage growing in independence since infancy will serve us well as we help them take the steps toward independence in safe social networking.

Levels of Risk on MySpace

The risks on MySpace can be categorized progressively. In chapter 15, we will look more closely at the risks and rewards of each level and how to tailor your limits to your child's individual maturity level. For now, here is a summary of the levels of risks as I see them:

Level 1: Communicating only with known friends with parental supervision. (No Events, No Forums, No Groups.)

Level 2: Communicating with known friends using guidelines given by parents but without constant parental supervision. (No Events, No Forums, No Groups.)

Level 3: Widening circle of friends to include people we do not know in real life, but still keeping profile set to private or friends only, still occasional parent safety checks of friends and content.

Level 4: Making oneself a public person by setting profile to public so that anyone can see your profile, reach your friends through your profile, and comment on your profile.

Level 5: Using MySpace to plan and coordinate live events, again with parental supervision, progressing toward adulthood, where this would be done without parental oversight.

Level 6: Venturing into forums, chat rooms, and groups where we do not know the people and will be exposed to their influence.

Level 7: Extreme danger! Entering forums, chat rooms, and unknown groups and reaching out in dangerous and provocative ways. Making oneself available as public, and even in person. Making profile public, sending out private information, sending out sexually provocative images, engaging in conversation with strangers on private, possibly sexually graphic topics, and using events in such a way that you can be easily located.

◄◄ ►►

The stories that make the papers usually take place in levels 6 and 7. When our teens tell us that our fears about their using MySpace are overblown, that may be accurate. However, by learning what MySpace includes and the growing risks our teens incur as their independence on MySpace grows, we will be better able to make distinctions that will allow them some measure of freedom while we also make sure they are practicing the skills they will need to stay safe online now and when they have grown up and are truly independent of our control.

Parent-Teen Power Struggles as They Grow toward Independence

Usually, the teenage years include some degree of power struggle between parents and teens. This naturally takes place as we try to navigate safely watching them grow in their independence. Generally speaking, teens are trying their wings, longing to be free to do as they please; they think they know pretty much everything they need to know and they yearn for independence.

Parents, however, are pulling on the reins to make sure they don't go too far too fast and end up in danger. They may be holding on too tightly or not paying enough attention. Teens want to be seen as capable of living their own lives (even though they still want us to provide dinner). So it's no wonder that there are times when life shared by parents and teens feels like a tug-of-war.

With regard to using MySpace and other social networking sites, they may feel intense pressure from their peers to participate and resent any hesitation on our part while we struggle to make sure they are safe. I hope that the overview of the stair steps toward greater independence on MySpace will help ease any parent-teen power struggles by giving you ways to manage the growing risks at each step along the way.

Why "No MySpace Ever" Won't Work

I anticipate that many readers may still be thinking, "No way!" One mom at a meeting for parents of teens, exclaimed, "No MySpace ever!" in response to the risks being presented. But as the group discussed our situation, we realized:

- Teens can have many social networking accounts with various free email addresses and user names.
- We can monitor the computer at home, but what if it's a laptop that can be moved?
- Even if we monitor our teens every moment at home, there's always the sleepover and peer pressure.
- They have access to social networking sites via hand-held wireless devices and high-tech cell phones.

As the parents group batted around our options, one mom blurted out, "This is overwhelming!" It may feel overwhelming, but we dare not just let ourselves be overwhelmed. We pressed on in the discussion to conclude that we needed to acknowledge that there is no getting around this with a simple "just say no" approach. We must go further than that, and I commend you for doing that right now.

Maybe This Is Bigger Than a "Yes!" or "No!"

A simple "yes" or "no" may not adequately deal with this new, immensely popular way of communicating that is overwhelming our culture. Instead of thinking in yes or no terms, it may be more helpful to think in terms of *if, how,* and/or *when* our teens will be allowed to use social networking, and *how to make sure they use it safely*. If social networking is confirmed as the preferred mode of communication (particularly among teens and young adults), there will come a time when our children will be grown and out of our homes. Then what? To declare an emphatic *No, not ever!* now will leave them to learn to navigate through this dangerous technology later on their own, without any supervision or awareness of the dangers.

If we just react with fear (and some degree of ignorance), we won't be of much help to them. Even if we end up deciding to limit their MySpace use, we will be much more productive if we understand how they see it and how important or pervasive it is to them, before we give our decree.

Maybe this parallel will evoke a sense of how it may feel to your teen when MySpace is simply forbidden. Consider these questions:

- How would you have felt—when you were a young teen—if your parents were convinced that using the telephone was too dangerous and forbade it?
- How would you have felt—as a senior in high school—if, after seeing the driver's training film *Red Asphalt*, your parents decided driving a car was far too dangerous and declared you would not drive, regardless of what your peers were doing?

These are fair comparisons from our teenage years to how some teens today feel about being banned from MySpace. In fact, the telephone analogy is grounded in credible research. According to the Pew Research Center—Internet and American Life Project, the correlation holds. In a generation, use of the Internet is likely to reach the same levels as that of the telephone, which is now used by 94 percent of Americans, or the television, which is used by 98 percent. This highlights the vital role the internet plays in the way our generation is choosing to communicate, and social networking will play a major role.

I hope these analogies also acknowledge that there are real dangers involved—serious dangers, as with driving—but that doesn't mean we declare our teens will never drive. We understand that driving is important enough in our society to warrant learning the skills to manage the dangers. As with the graduated steps toward independence in life, it's not so much the level of risk as how one manages the risk at each level, and how one conducts interaction with others at that level, that determines one's overall safety.

Undoubtedly driving has a built-in degree of danger. If our teen has learned to drive safely, there is still danger, but it's worth the risk. Whom our teens are driving *with* and the way they conduct themselves either increases or lessens the risks. Drinking and driving or racing the car causes the danger to spike precipitously.

When it comes to social networking, we must see its importance to our teen along with its *real* dangers—not the impression we've gotten via media hype. Then we can decide how best to help our teen navigate life in this age of technological advancements as he or she moves into adulthood. That's not to say that any particular teen *should* be allowed to go on MySpace or another social networking site just because "everyone else is doing it." However, it does illustrate the importance of what you are doing now by using this book to gain enough knowledge to make informed decisions.

Build a Wall or Suit Them with Armor?

I think every concerned parent of teens living in this day and age is influenced by fear for our teen's safety, whether we show it or not. This is a scary time to be raising teens, although also an exciting time. I see the attempt to keep our teens safe falling into two general metaphorical categories.

Building Walls

One approach is to focus our attention and energies on trying to build walls to keep them safely in where we can personally protect them. This approach involves lots of limits that contribute to safety. However, there is a problem with this approach that parents of teens realize all too well. When we build a wall, it seems to evoke a desire within our teen to escape those boundaries. So parents may end up doing guard duty round the clock, and since we can't stay with them 24–7, they have opportunities to escape our imposed protections.

In dealing with the MySpace situation, any walls we build can be scaled by our teen's technological superiority. No matter how impressive the limits we put on them or what monitoring software we choose, they can get around it if they put their minds to it. When asked about use of monitoring software to track teens' internet use, Joanne McNabb of the California Office of Privacy Protection replied, "Whether or not you use monitoring software or spyware to track your teen's internet use depends on your relationship and the trustworthiness of the teen. However, the best safety option is open communication with your teen. Monitoring software can be helpful, but it is never a substitute for parental commitment and involvement."[1]

To my way of thinking, the build-a-wall-and-keep-them-in approach with teens wanting to use social networking—no matter how big the wall and how sophisticated the surveillance—is similar to building the equivalent of the Great Wall of China but discovering our teens can fly an airplane and their friends have access to one. In this case, walls are not enough.

Walls Are Not Enough

This is not just my opinion. I made a point of pursuing this question with every expert I met at the Cyber-Safety Summit. I found many who are working diligently to get parents to join them in educating teens to protect themselves online, but not one of them suggested that the answer to the dangers presented by social networking was to forbid it. Not one! The experts are trying to get us parents to be the chief security officer for our own teens. They also are trying to get us to realize that we and our teens would be better off if we put our energy into helping them develop the protective armor they can carry on their person and take with them out into the world.

Infancy was the time for the crib, the toddler years required a playpen, the kindergarten playground and schoolyard needed a fence; however—according to cyber-safety experts—the teenage years in an age of social networking via the internet are better served by suiting our teens with metaphorical armor rather than reinforcing our walls and fences.

The armor they need is good sense, knowledge, and wisdom gained from growing in independence under the watchful supervision of parents who are learning what's going on with social networking and the internet. The cyber-safety experts want parents to make sure that their teens are learning the safety skills they need at each stage of their growth toward independence online so that they can become responsible MySpace citizens and good neighbors to everyone they meet on the World Wide Web.

If Not You, Who? If Not Now, When?

The Talmud poses the question, "If not you, who? If not now, when?" This is something we should ponder as it applies to social networking and MySpace. As our teens are growing toward greater and greater independence, who will teach them the skills they need to stay safe? When will they learn these skills that are essential in this generation? If we do not begin to allow them to learn the basics of social networking under our supervision, when will they learn it? When they go off to college? If we are not the ones guiding them in this important area of interacting with their world, who will?

It may not be time yet for your teen to venture into social networking; you are the best one to decide when the time is right. But please bear in mind that the good judgment our teens need to develop to become safe social networkers must be practiced. All the experts agree that practice is best done under the direction of a caring mom or dad. Once teens see that you are working with them to help them grow toward responsible online independence, the parent-teen power struggle can become creative collaboration. Our fears of their venturing away from us and into dangerous areas on MySpace can be replaced with becoming proud of them for the way they are learning to manage the risks at every step along the way.

13

Should *My* Teen
Use MySpace?

Should *my* teen use MySpace? This is a question only you can answer, and the answer may be different for each of your teens if you have more than one. There's plenty to consider when making this decision. As I've talked with many parents I've heard various comments like these:

- "MySpace looks like a huge time waster. My daughter is busy enough with homework, music, sports practice, and church events. Why add more?"
- "My son is a huge flirt. I'm afraid he'd use MySpace just to check out girls and lead them on."

The most powerful response came from family members — one of my sisters (Dianna) and her husband (Bud), both of whom made me pause and rethink the decision I've made to let my two teens participate on MySpace. I asked my family in particular because I knew they would not pull any punches with me. Here's that they said that made me reconsider *my* teen's use of MySpace (although I reserved the right to weigh the risks and rewards and make my own decision, as should you). Bud wrote:

> Have you lost your mind???….Whoops, Blunt Bud strikes again. I'll see if I can say it another way. Child raising, protecting, and tutoring are not and should never be an exercise in blind fairness and blind compassion toward a peer. Our children, no matter how intelligent and mature they may seem, ARE CHILDREN!!! The internet arena is a wonderful thing if one has a lick of sense and a modicum of restraint. Children, lacking experience in life or business, usually have neither. Pedophiles and salespeople are well aware of this and LOVE it!

Case in point: Taylor is surfing MySpace and tells his love of music and God. A little "web-cam" posing and some perverted clown with a good line, a guitar and a Bible sees that red hair, exuberance, and baby face and thinks, "This kid is mine!"

Case in point: Mom is gone shopping and Haley swaps pictures and info with "a very NICE boy." (She can't tell that this NICE boy is really a twenty-five-year-old rapist who is "surfing" for his next victim.) This nice "boy" has been doing this for years. He's a great con. He knows how to work the female mind AND he is dealing with a young girl who is on the verge of becoming a young woman. He thinks, "THIS GIRL IS MINE!"

Hey Connie, if your kids are on the internet, be apprehensive, careful, and watchful. There are better places for them to interact with peers and have fun doing it. Dianna speaks to this below. See ya Connie. Good luck.

Dianna's views followed:

MySpace should not be necessary if our children are involved with school, sports, church, and family. I feel our children should not open themselves up to God-knows-what or WHO, just for the sake of entertainment. They are learning to read people in everyday life, which can be hard. Just imagine how hard it would be to know when someone on the internet has an ulterior motive. All children are different, but they have the basic need of being liked. Even adults have been taken for rides over the internet. Everyday, new schemes are developed just to use people for someone else's gratification; most of the time this is not for the good. How can we expect our children and grandchildren do what we ourselves cannot do, protect ourselves against predators?

So, should *your* teen be on MySpace. This is not a decision to be taken lightly. There are serious ramifications and serious safety concerns to be weighted out. And you are the only one who can make that decision and weigh out the risks versus rewards for your family. I commend you for daring to do so and encourage you as you continue. Later in this book, I break down the progressive increments of dangers and safety precautions required for each one. Hopefully this will help you make a wise and safe decision for each of the teens you love and who are under your authority.

Judging from the parents I've listened to and quizzed about this, most have a host of valid reasons for strong hesitations about their teen using MySpace. Most of the teens I've talked with whose parents prohibit them from MySpace have a litany of valid reasons for why they want to go on MySpace. Most have given the dangers careful thought and believe they have the good sense to stay safe on a social networking site. Whether they really do or not remains to be seen.

We've spent most of the book thus far learning about MySpace and why it is so appealing for teens in general. Now I'd like you to zero in on why *your* teen wants to use MySpace. I suggest that you and your teen exchange views and consider each other's points of concern. You may think your teen won't participate, but if your permission to use MySpace or willingness to consider easing up restrictions is contingent on being persuaded, your teen might find that motivation enough to enter into an exchange of views.

Experience It Online!

If you want to get the full experience, you can go to *www.MySpace. com/momsanddads* and check my blog for this chapter. There you can find out how you can do this exercise with your teen *via* MySpace while you're swapping views *about* MySpace. I'll show you how to set up your profile and your teen's so that only the two of you can see what you are communicating. If you want to go the noncomputer route, you can write letters.

Ask, and Be Prepared to Listen

If your teen believes that you are open to being persuaded, the invitation to lay out his reasons for wanting to have a MySpace page may hold appeal. However, often communication between parents and teens gets cut off by one interrupting the other to present their point of view or counter with an argument. Remember that line from an old Cat Stevens song, "From the moment I could talk, I was ordered to listen." No one likes that kind of conversation, and it rarely results in much hearing and understanding.

Your teen will need some assurance that he or she will be fully heard. This can be one of the benefits of communicating via the com-

puter or MySpace; people can swap points of view without being inter-
rupted. So try promising that if your teen will write out his reasons for
wanting to be on MySpace, you will genuinely consider the possibility,
but you have to finish figuring out what you need to know before you
can decide.

I suggested this exercise to a close-knit family from our church—
mom, dad, one teen daughter, and one teen son—who were troubled
about MySpace. As I began work on this book, the mom, Julie, con-
fided that MySpace is the *only* issue that causes their family recurrent
conflict. The daughter, Piper, is almost seventeen, an excellent student
and extremely well behaved; in short, she's a parent's dream of what
parenting a teen should be. Piper's parents have not allowed her to
have a MySpace page even though that is where most of her friends
connect.

When they heard I was working on this book, Julie showed interest
and Piper sent word that she hoped I could get through to her mom and
dad where she had failed to get through. Given their common interest, expressed to me by each one privately, I asked Julie and Piper to
write their reasons: Piper, her reasons for wanting to go on MySpace;
Julie, her reasons for not wanting Piper to go on MySpace. I share these
insights with their permission.

After you read their letters, write out your own reasons for hesitat-
ing about or prohibiting MySpace. Ask your teen to write out why he
or she wants to use social networking. The key is neither to interrupt
each other's thoughts nor to deride them. Your aim at this point in the
process should be to fully consider, respect, and try to understand the
other person's concerns. If it feels too weird to write each other a letter,
you can both pretend you are explaining your reasons to me and write
the letter to me; it worked for Julie and Piper.

Mom's Letter

Dear Connie,

*Please use this information as you will. I am looking forward to
hearing and reading your thoughts on the subject of MySpace. I realize
that many teens are using it now, but I have real concerns about it,
and it is probably the most divisive topic of conversation in our house
these days.*

Let me start by saying that my daughter, Piper, is a wonderful person. She has a great head on her shoulders; she has a strong faith and a heart for helping others. We know her friends and their families and they are loving people with similar ideas about life in general. This may be part of my problem with MySpace. As a MySpace user she will have the impact of many more teens' opinions. I am confident that teens do what their friends do. For instance, if you find a group of teens who all smoke and your child is one of their best buddies, the odds are greater that your child will smoke. When Piper was starting junior high, she had friends who had a lot more freedom than her; they were more aggressive and mean-spirited. It was the only time in our relationship that Piper was mean-spirited and fought with us about being treated like a child. Later, as her group of friends changed to others who were more like her and had boundaries more in line with the ones we impose, life got easier for all of us and she was happier. Does MySpace expand your circle of friends in healthy or unhealthy ways?

My friend's daughter has a MySpace profile, so my friend decided to go on every once in a while to see what the kids are saying. She was shocked by the talk of sex, drugs, and alcohol, and the general meanness expressed by her daughter's teammates and their friends. Her daughter is another put-together girl, so she was surprised. Her closest friends were not as mean or wild in their writings, but now, through MySpace, her daughter is bringing home all of that garbage from people that she would see occasionally at school or at sporting events. Whether the sex, drugs, and alcohol are real or just the bragging of fakers, it still has an impact on what our teens perceive their peers are doing.

Both of the high schools that my children attend have sent home strong warnings about monitoring the use of MySpace. Why? Clearly there is some cause for concern. They speak of cyber bullying and bringing the meanness of the playground into the home. For many kids, home is their sanctuary against bullying, but now the bullies can get at them where they live. The bullies also can spread rumors to a larger audience. This is not my concern for Piper in particular, but it is a concern I have with MySpace in general.

When you hear about teens using MySpace, you hear about predators. Piper insists that she would have a private MySpace and only let those in that she knows. I think that is wise. I also think that hackers and people out to do harm keep working at ways of getting through to victims. How do you stay ahead of those whose goal it is to get to you? Her friends all have phony names and stats. Clearly, putting your information out into cyberspace is not a wise move. Kids are tricked all the time into saying, and now writing, more than they intend. Just the need for secrecy gets my radar up.

Teens are writing things now that they will find silly or downright destructive later in life. Already people in public positions must defend things they emailed in the early nineties when they were young that they would never say now. I think that what is written will be out there for a long time, and this archive alone of teen stupidity may come back to haunt many of these kids. I know I wouldn't want to defend my thoughts or actions from high school or college. Once you write something on the computer, it is out there.

My last thought is for Piper in particular. She is a great student who spends a lot of time studying. While she studies, her mind wanders and she checks email or looks online for clothing, and so on. I am concerned that for a person whose time is so limited and who is so involved at church and school, the time spent on MySpace will be coming from time she does not have to spare. I would love for her to be less busy and not so involved in so many things, but I'm not sure that's in the cards for Piper. As it is, her plate is too full, and there doesn't seem as though there is room for anything else.

You said to write this from the heart, so I haven't taken the time to write this in any particular order of importance to have the greatest impact. This is not something I want to win by being persuasive. I feel that the book you are writing will help many of us who struggle with MySpace. I look forward to guidance from you. In our house, we don't like it when one wins and the other loses. We strive for solutions that work for the good of the whole family. It isn't easy, but it is a goal that keeps us together.

God bless you as you take on this huge task.
Julie

P.S. Piper and I made a point of not reading each other's emails to you. She was very excited about hers and the ideas it brought up. Even though we have talked this thing to death, I think it will be a very healthy exercise for us to read each other's thoughts.

Teen's Letter

Dear Mrs. Neal,

First of all, thanks for supporting the cause! Here is my argument in the attempt to make MySpace an open option for those who are without.

First off, I acknowledge the fact that MySpace is often abused and that dangerous things have resulted from lack of caution. But I also acknowledge that MySpace is a great form of communication that is currently sweeping the nation. The first thing my parents said when I brought up the subject was "Why don't you just use email or instant messaging?" Even though these two forms of communication are great and very useful, MySpace adds different components: quick conversation and personality. Instant messenger allows quick conversation, but the chances of both typers being on line at the same time are so slim, even more so as school schedules become more demanding. Also, MySpace allows expression through music, pictures, video clips, etc.

This brings us to the next issue addressed by parents: "It is dangerous to have information about yourself on the World Wide Web!" I see this point and see the dangers that MySpace presents. However, there are many ways to make MySpace safe. The most obvious would be to set your MySpace to private. This prevents anyone not classified as a "friend" from seeing it. Once a friend is added, they can see and comment on the profile as much as they want.

This issue also brings up the topic of meeting people online. My only response is: I hope that my parents trust me and trust their parenting enough to know that my knowledge of safety precautions regarding information on the internet is more than sufficient. I am aware of the fact that there are people who "meet" on the internet, and I am also aware that these people can often times be dangerous; so why would I be compelled to talk to them?

Throughout the years, I have lost contact with many friends. Since I have no knowledge of their email address and since it would be awkward to call for no apparent reason, the acquaintance seems lost for good. However, MySpace provides an advantageous and easy way to reconnect. This is probably the most appealing to me at the moment, since my curiosity as to how old friends are doing is increasing. With

MySpace, it would be extremely simple to "search" for someone and then restart the friendship (as long as their MySpace was not private).

Lastly, MySpace is simply a fun way to communicate with friends. Although this reason is not the most persuasive, it is still the reason why most teens want to use MySpace. I have had many friends tell me that when they move away, or go to college, they will mainly keep in touch with friends on MySpace for the sheer simplicity of it. MySpace is basically the "new email" and is extremely appealing when it is the main way communication is carried out (close second to talking, of course).

Thanks for hearing me out! Hopefully this provides some enlightenment for parents — and a little oomph for the teen argument!

If any more information is needed or I failed to mention a topic, please let me know and I will be glad to email again!

Thanks
Piper

P.S. MySpace is an awesome way to talk to that guy you always see in math class but can't get up the courage to call!

Julie and Piper both presented their concerns well. Hopefully the exchange of letters has carried their conversation forward. Let's try something else to help you move your conversation forward with your teen. Write your letter — either on paper or on the computer — and ask your teen to do the same. Then swap letters, read, consider, and wait for twenty-four hours before discussing what was written.

Why Do You Like MySpace (Or Think You Would If Allowed)?

The MySpace experience differs according to the interests of each user, so it helps to know why your teen likes it and how each individual plans to use it. In our house, Haley uses it mostly for visiting and sharing her life with her wide circle of friends from church and school, planning events, passing notes, sharing photo logs of our vacations, promoting and raising funds for her mission trips, seeing what's happening at her youth group, and sharing music she loves.

Our son, Taylor, is focused on promoting his music as a singer/song-writer/performer.[1] He uses MySpace to send out announcements about his upcoming gigs and concerts. He can invite friends, get an RSVP, have his friends invite their friends to hear him play, and make his music available for anyone to hear—including Grandma, who lives hours away and is too infirm to attend his performances. Immediately after a concert, he can check his MySpace page to get feedback from his audience, friends, and fans. He also sends notes and messages to friends, but much less than Haley does.

Your goal is to find out why *your teen* loves MySpace and how he or she would use it or already uses it. Maybe your teen isn't the letter-writing type and answers your question "Why?" with a grunt. Okay, see if your teen will complete a survey by reading each statement and circling the number that best describes how important that aspect of social networking is to him or her. If your teen doesn't use a social networking site, ask him or her to anticipate which would be most important.

▷ Ask Your Teen

How would you use MySpace? How much does this feature of MySpace matter to you?

0 = This is not important to me at all; I don't or wouldn't use that feature.

1 = This feature is not very important to me, although I have used it or might use it occasionally.

2 = This feature is okay; I do use it or would probably use it.

3 = This feature is very important to me, I do or would definitely use it because ...

Circle one number. Use blank lines provided to fill in your reasons for using a certain feature.

0 1 2 3   To communicate with friends I already know and see regularly.

_____

0 1 2 3   To communicate with people in my family.

_____

0 1 2 3   To send and receive instant messages.

0 1 2 3   To check out peers without being seen (by visiting personal profiles).

0 1 2 3   To keep in touch with friends who live far away.

0 1 2 3   To express my changing moods and how I'm feeling (mood icons and words) so friends can know.

0 1 2 3   To "try out" various personas by representing myself in different ways at different times and see how others react.

0 1 2 3   To express myself creatively or artistically in (circle all that apply) music, comedy, video, film, writing, poetry, photography, other.

0 1 2 3   To get feedback (kudos and comments) from others about my artistic or creative expression.

0 1 2 3   To find out what events are happening or what plans are taking shape.

0 1 2 3   To get details about events: see who's going to be there, location, directions, time, etc.

0 1 2 3   To explore the ideas of others on a topic of interest.

0 1 2 3   To check out people I sort of know, but want to know better by looking at profiles of classmates, friends, and friends of friends.

_____

0 1 2 3   To flirt.

_____

0 1 2 3   To "meet" or "talk to" someone in my school or real-life social circle I'm hesitant to approach in person.

_____

0 1 2 3   To see where I fit in and find a place to belong in groups or clubs.

_____

0 1 2 3   To see how many "friends" I can collect.

_____

0 1 2 3   To "meet" new people I don't know in real life who look interesting or share my interests.

_____

0 1 2 3   To make a positive difference in the world by making my presence known and getting people to join me in reaching a worthy goal.

_____

0 1 2 3   To connect or communicate with a specific—limited—group to focus on a shared interest or project (this could be a group related to religion, hobbies, a school project, or a class homework project).

0 1 2 3   Other use for MySpace:

_____

0 1 2 3   Other use for MySpace:

_____

Arrange a conversation with your teen where you can move from just reading each other's letters to hearing each other's voices. Use these discussion starters to help get the conversation going:

1. Take turns sharing something new you learned from the other's letter.
2. Look over the survey and note which items your teen indicated as a #3: "This feature is very important to me because ..." Have your teen explain why that feature is important and some of the others are not as important. Listen.

Perhaps your teen has convinced you that she has valid reasons for wanting to use MySpace. If so, the next step is to determine her awareness of safety issues on MySpace, and also to educate yourself further about MySpace safety. That's the topic of the next chapter.

14

Basic Safety Tips
for MySpace

Remember the comforting scenes from early sitcoms where the mom—usually home baking some heavenly confection—pushed back the curtain of the kitchen window to look out and make sure the kids playing outside were okay? Those were the days—back when kids were safe to play outside, before parents started keeping them inside more for fear they might be snatched or lured into some harmful activity by a passing stranger.

Whether the mom was Donna Reed, Harriet Nelson, June Cleaver, or even Mrs. Wilson (checking to see what Dennis the Menace was doing), we felt safer knowing there was someone always there to be looking out for the kids in our neighborhood. Those were the days when father knew best! If trouble was brewing, it wasn't long before one of the moms or dads was out the door to make sure all mischief stopped before anyone got hurt.

Well, the neighborhood has changed. Instead of playing on the corner lot in the neighborhood near our homes, many teens now live, play, relate, and build connections in online neighborhoods. These may correspond to a real group at their school, sports team, or church, or they may be made up of people from all over the world who share an interest. Still, our teens need someone metaphorically looking out the window to make sure they are okay. That's our responsibility! It's nice that MySpace and some of the other major social networking sites have put people on staff to cover their part of the responsibility, but no one can replace our role if we fail to fulfill our responsibility. If there's a problem, our teens need someone aware enough, savvy enough, and motivated enough to step in to thwart the danger. That's us!

Finding Up-to-Date Safety Tips on MySpace

You will find the link to the latest safety tips in the menu bar at the very bottom of any MySpace page. Practice finding these safety tips and review them periodically to see whether anything has changed. On the following page are the tips for users and for parents given by MySpace as of this writing.

Safety Tips

MySpace makes it easy to express yourself, connect with friends and make new ones, but please remember that what you post publicly could embarrass you or expose you to danger. Here are some common-sense guidelines that you should follow when using MySpace:

Safety Tips   **myspace.com**®
                                                                   a place for friends

| Safety Tips | Tips For Parents |

MySpace makes it easy to express yourself, connect with friends and make new ones, but please remember that what you post publicly could embarrass you or expose you to danger. Here are some common sense guidelines that you should follow when using MySpace:

- **Don't forget that your profile and MySpace forums are public spaces.** Don't post anything you wouldn't want the world to know (e.g., your phone number, address, IM screens name, or specific whereabouts). Avoid posting anything that would make it easy for a stranger to find you, such as where you hang out every day after school.
- **People aren't always who they say they are. Be careful about adding strangers to your friends list.** It's fun to connect with new MySpace friends from all over the world, but avoid meeting people in person whom you do not fully know. If you must meet someone, do it in a public place and bring a friend or trusted adult.
- **Harassment, hate speech and inappropriate content should be reported.** If you feel someone's behavior is inappropriate, react. Talk with a trusted adult, or report it to MySpace or the authorities.
- **Don't post anything that would embarrass you later.** Think twice before posting a photo or info you wouldn't want your parents or boss to see!
- **Don't mislead people into thinking that you're older or younger.** If you are under 14 and pretend to be older, customer service will delete your profile. If you are over 18 and pretend to be a teenager to contact underage users, customer service will delete your profile.
- **Don't get hooked by a phishing scam.** Phishing is a method used by fraudsters to try to get your personal information, such as your username and password, by pretending to be a site you trust. Click here to learn more.

MySpace Tips for Parents

For teens, MySpace is a popular online hangout because the site makes it easy for them to express themselves and keep in touch with their friends.

As a parent, please consider the following guidelines to help your children make safe decisions about using online communities.[2]

Safety Tips   **myspace.com®**
                                                      a place for friends

| Safety Tips | Tips For Parents |

For teens, MySpace is a popular online hangout because the site makes it easy for them to express themselves and keep in touch with their friends.

As a parent, please consider the following guidelines to help your children make safe decisions about using online communities.

- **Talk to your kids about why they use MySpace, how they communicate with others and how they represent themselves on MySpace.**
- **Kids shouldn't lie about how old they are. MySpace members must be 14 years of age or older.** We take extra precautions to protect our younger members and we are not able to do so if they do not identify themselves as such. MySpace will delete users whom we find to be younger than 14, or those misrepresenting their age.
- **MySpace is a public space.** Members shouldn't post anything they wouldn't want the world to know (e.g., phone number, address, IM screen name, or specific whereabouts). Tell your children they should avoid posting anything that would make it easy for a stranger to find them, such as their local hangouts.
- **Remind them not to post anything that could embarrass them later or expose them to danger.** Although MySpace is public, teens sometimes think that adults can't see what they post. Tell them that they shouldn't post photos or info they wouldn't want adults to see.
- **People aren't always who they say they are. Ask your children to be careful about adding strangers to their friends list.** It's fun to connect with new MySpace friends from all over the world, but members should be cautious when communicating with people they don't know. They should talk to you if they want to meet an online friend in person, and if you think it's safe, any meeting should take place in public and with friends or a trusted adult present.
- **Harassment, hate speech and inappropriate content should be reported.** If your kids encounter inappropriate behavior, let them know that they can let you know, or they should report it to MySpace or the authorities.
- **Don't get hooked by a phishing scam.** Phishing is a method used by fraudsters to try to get your personal information, such as your username and password, by pretending to be a site you trust. Click here to learn more.

Click Here to remove your child's profile from MySpace

For more information on Monitoring software, please visit:

- Software4parents.com
- k9webprotection.com
- SafeFamilies.org

Ask Your Teen

If your teen is already on MySpace or wants to join, go over these safety tips with her, or have her go over them and think through how they are to be applied. Then have her answer the following questions. Her answers will let you know what degree of understanding and caution she has regarding social networking. You may be pleased to discover that your teen is careful to follow and apply all of these, or you may realize that your teen is clueless and needs direction. (Checking their answers against the safety tips will also reinforce the application for you.) I've provided blank lines in case you'd like to jot down your teen's answers.

To get the best results, tell your teen that your aim is to become assured that he or she is interacting safely and responsibly so that you can reduce your level of monitoring. The more they cooperate as you go through this process, the sooner you will loosen your grip, if they earn your trust.

1. What precautions should you take because you understand that your profile and MySpace forums are public spaces?

   _____

   _____

2. What kinds of clues or information should you be careful *not* to put on MySpace? Why?

   _____

   _____

3. Suppose a stranger sees you on MySpace and finds you interesting and wants to find you or meet you in person. How would you handle that situation?

   _____

   _____

4. What risks are involved in meeting someone you initially "meet" online?

   _____

   _____

5. Under what circumstance might you think it was okay to plan to meet someone in person whom you initially met online?

_____

_____

6. What kinds of things are deemed "inappropriate content" on MySpace? What kinds of content would you deem inappropriate enough to cause you to delete a comment someone left on your profile page?

_____

_____

7. What would you do, have you done, or do you plan to do when you encounter inappropriate content or communication that makes you uncomfortable? (If you are going to be on a social networking site, you must be prepared.)

_____

_____

8. What are proper ways to react if you encounter what you think *might* be inappropriate content?

_____

_____

9. Which person would you least like to have view your most embarrassing photo or read your most embarrassing post? (Maybe Grandma, your youth pastor, or Dad.) If you currently have a profile page, check it and delete anything that you wouldn't want that person to see.

_____

_____

10. What might be the consequences if you mislead people into thinking that you are older or younger than your true age?

_____

_____

11. What age must you be to honestly be a MySpace member? Why might you say that you are "100 years old," and do you think that is okay?

_____

_____

12. What is a "phishing scam" and how would you know if you were being targeted? How can you avoid becoming a victim of a phishing scam?

_____

_____

This conversation with your teen may put your mind at ease. If so, that's great. The ultimate goal is to know he or she is well prepared to interact safely online. However, if your teen is lacking in the knowledge needed to stay safe online, suggest to him or her that demonstrating such skills will go a long way toward convincing you to give them greater online freedom.

Exploring Hyperlinks to Off-Site Safety Sites

Not only does MySpace offer safety tips, it makes available contact information to other organizations that can help you learn more to keep your teen safe. It's good to know how to use the hyperlinks, which appear as highlighted text on the Safety Tips and Tips for Parents pages of MySpace. While most organizations rely on websites to make their information available, pages 208–209 will also give you phone numbers and street addresses of a few highly respected organizations committed to educating parents in ways to keep their kids and teens safe online.

Hyperlinks work basically the same most places on the internet. When you see text in color or highlighted, point your cursor at it and click. It should take you to more information about that point or take you to the website address listed. For example, in the Safety Tips page at this time, the point "Don't get hooked by a phishing scam" is followed by a highlighted "*Click here* to learn more." By pointing your cursor on "Click here" and clicking, you will be taken to a page that will fully explain a "phishing scam." There also may be a list of other resources given that you are encouraged to visit with hyperlinks.

A Computer Game That Teaches Internet Safety

One of the remote sites you may be led to is Web Wise Kids, listed on page 209 in this book, with resources that allow your teen to play their way to safer internet interaction. They have developed teen-tested video games that work much better than a lecture at teaching teens internet safety skills while also motivating them.

For example, the computer game *Missing* is designed for middle-school children (ages 11 to 15) and has been used by over one million children. It is based on a true story of a teenager who meets a predator online and is lured away from home. Players take on the role of a police detective, examining chat-room conversations between Zack and his new "friend" Fantasma, looking for clues to find Zack and bring him home. Fun and engaging, *Missing* also teaches teens how to use the internet and sites like MySpace safely.[3]

Make It Safe for Your Teen to Come to You

Several times on the Safety Tips page it mentions that teens should talk to a trusted adult if they are having problems on MySpace or online. This is very important. You and I need to be or become that trusted adult in our teen's life. If our teens think that the result of telling us about a problem will be to lose internet privileges or be banned from social networking, most teens will take their risks online rather than risk being cut off.

The 2001 Girl Scout research report *The Net Effect: Girls and New Media*, based on the internet experiences of 1,246 girls ages thirteen to eighteen, showed that 30 percent encountered some form of sexual harassment in a chat room, but only 7 percent of those told a parent.

The research report states:

> The hesitancy to tell parents about harassment appears to stem from a fear that parents will overreact and ban girls from socializing on-line. For this reason most girls keep quiet about online harassment unless it is really scary. Thus if adults want girls to come to them when they have frightening online experiences, they need to create an environment in which girls do not feel that they will be blamed or punished for sexual harassment that is not their fault.[4]

The report further states that with respect to online activities, girls want parents to:

- Teach them to have responsibility.
- Educate them about possible dangers.
- Be cautious but not too cautious.
- Trust them.[5]

Therefore, we would do well to focus on building trust in our relationship with our teens, keep communication open, and listen carefully to their input regarding online safety.

I realize that some of you may be thinking, it's fine and good to talk about building trust, but what if my teen has earned my distrust? That situation does arise, and when it does, parents need to follow the tactics of President Ronald Reagan when he was trying to build a better relationship with the Soviet Union: *Trust, but verify!*

I'll close out this chapter by going over some of the technological ways we can verify the truth of what our teens are doing online.

An Overview of Monitoring Software Options

Monitoring software helps you watch over your teen's Web use. There are various levels of monitoring and various philosophical and relational approaches represented by each. I see three basic categories you may want to consider:

Spying Software

Software4Parents is a type of spying software. It can secretly record MySpace, email, chat, IM, blogs, and even passwords. I recommend you not employ this option except in the most extreme circumstance. Spying tends to undermine the open communication that is needed to grow trust between parent and child.

Filtering and Guidance Software

This kind of monitoring software doesn't spy on every site visited and every keystroke; rather, it helps your family steer clear of the most dangerous kinds of internet sites that one can get to purposely or accidentally from MySpace, including pornographic sites. K9 Web Protection is a service that operates in this way and was featured on the MySpace safety page. They describe themselves as a "guide dog"—hence the K9 ("canine") reference in their name—"to help protect your family and keep them out of dangerous internet 'neighborhoods.'" Thus they stop short of spying.

Social Networking Reporting Software

Another form of monitoring service is represented by BeNetSafe.com, which describes their services as follows: "BeNetSafe™ Internet security software monitors your kids' friends and content on MySpace and Xanga ... You will be alerted with detailed reports indicating any potentially dangerous or reckless behavior."

For our purposes right now, be assured that if you decide you need help monitoring what your teen is doing on social networking sites, there is a range of software and services that can help you, once you decide your aim and philosophy regarding keeping tabs on your teen.

Get Ready to Go on Duty in Your Teen's MySpace Neighborhood

Once again let's recall those wise moms and dads from the fifties and sixties family sitcoms. Mom always managed to stay discretely hidden behind the curtains while making sure the neighborhood was safe, and Dad took action to protect his family but managed to speak to his teens in private so they wouldn't be embarrassed in front of their friends. Those are good role models to follow.

To make the MySpace neighborhood a safer place without even letting your teen know you are looking out from behind the metaphorical curtain, be certain to report any abuse or harassment, inappropriate content, and any crimes or potential crimes. You provide a service to MySpace and its users by reporting any such inappropriate content. According to a handout I received at the California Cyber-Safety Summit from MySpace, "MySpace's current procedures include providing a link on every page to (1) the Terms of Use, (2) the Privacy Policy, (3) Safety Tips, and (4) Contact MySpace, which presents an easy way for users to report 'abuse' on the site, including identifying 'underage users' and 'inappropriate content.' Inappropriate content includes both the verbal and image arenas."[6]

MySpace actually relies on users to help them locate inappropriate content so they can quickly remove it. The above-mentioned handout states (boldface added):

> MySpace is diligent in reviewing its site for inappropriate content, reviewing each image, photo, video, and classified that is uploaded to the MySpace server for compliance with the Terms of Use and Photo Policy. MySpace has also already begun reviewing images that are linked on third-party servers. In addition, we engage and rely on our users to assist us with this task by providing our users with methods to inform us of content that violates MySpace policies. **At the bottom of each profile page there is a link to "Report Inappropriate Content" so users can report any profile with questionable content.**
>
> MySpace personnel investigate these reports, and if an image on the website violates the Terms of Use, the Photo Policy, or is otherwise deemed inappropriate, the image and possibly the entire profile are deleted. The MySpace staff will, as warranted by the circumstances, additionally investigate the user's friends to ascertain patterns of violations and identify and remove further inappropriate content.[7]

This concludes the general safety precautions all parents of teens should make sure are in place. But the most important "place" for keeping your teen safe isn't on a page on MySpace. Proverbs 4:23 admonishes us, "Above all else, guard your heart, for it is the wellspring of life." Therefore, we need to focus on helping our teens learn to guard their own heart, what enters it, and what flows from it through MySpace. This ultimately will contribute a great deal to keeping them safe.

15

Risks versus Rewards: Deciding Where to Draw the Lines

If I were going to ask someone for directions around MySpace, I'd go to a big, burly, but kind-faced police officer. I found just such a man at an information booth for the Internet Crimes against Children Task Force (ICAC) at the California Cyber-Safety Summit. His name is Officer Jan Hoganson, and he works for the Sacramento sheriff's office, tracking online predators and educating parents and the public about internet safety, among other things.

I asked Officer Hoganson, "Do you think there is a safe way for teens to use MySpace?"

His answer surprised me. "Sure! Teens are going to gather somewhere, at the mall or at MySpace. Either place has its dangers. At least with MySpace you can monitor them." He too was one of the experts espousing the philosophy that "the most powerful person in the room is an involved parent."

As noted before, most decisions about MySpace don't fall neatly into a yes or no decision. If you choose to let your teen participate on social networking sites, whether MySpace or any other social networking sites (including Christian ones), realize that social networking offers and represents a continuum of life choices that need to be monitored and graduated according to what you know about your teen, your family's values, your teen's level of maturity, and your teen's ability to demonstrate responsible and safe online/interpersonal behavior.

The following series of graduated choices cover the continuum of using MySpace from starting as a non-MySpace registrant just checking out the MySpace home page, through areas where the rewards can outweigh the risks (depending on the teen), on into the danger zone where risks far outweigh any possible rewards.

As we begin weighing the rewards against the risks of using MySpace, my teens brought something to my attention that bears repeating for your sake. Many of the risks and rewards found on MySpace are also encountered in real life. Whenever teens go to a public place or watch mass media, they run risks of encountering things that don't mesh with our values. Our teens practice making choices and "screening out" objectionable material throughout the course of their day.

One of the rewards I see for us as parents is that MySpace delineates and magnifies the issues and influences our teens are having to learn to manage. If we can see these laid out on MySpace, it gives us greater opportunity to add our influence or to help them learn to manage life as it comes at them, even the parts of life we wish were not bombarding us (such as ads or TV commercials).

Level One

Going to *www.myspace.com*.

Rewards

Access to information about MySpace; Safety Tips; link to Contact MySpace to report abuse, inappropriate content, or underage users; power of the Interests Box—including helpful information, like being able to find movies and show times in your area instantly, access to some items on menu bar (Browse; Forums; Groups; Events—find only, not create; Music; Videos; Comedy; Film).

Risks

Might see ads you dislike; if your teen chooses to follow hyperlinks in the menu bar or interests box it could lead to material you deem inappropriate. Browsing can lead to MySpace member profiles set to public, which may include offensive language, photos, music, or content.

Where Do You Draw the Line for Your Teen?

Don't go there.	Go but don't become a member.	Go, but choose links wisely.	Okay to go and sign up.

Draw the line somewhere on the continuum above for your teen at this time.

Level Two

Registering as a MySpace member, but keeping profile set to "private" and limiting "friends" to people already known and approved of by parents.

Rewards

Able to search for and access good content in previously restricted areas.

Able to communicate with select group of "friends," share information, music, photos, videos for a good purpose, if so chosen.

Free to create and contribute positive content that could have positive influence in terms of image, perception by "friends," or impact on friends who have access to your teen's profile.

Able to communicate with any other MySpace member who has their profile set to public, using any of the communication tools available on every profile page, and to manage contact from other MySpace members (including the ability to block any user from contacting you on MySpace or leaving comments).

Able to send a bulletin to all your "friends" at once.

Able to receive bulletins from those who have added you to their "friends" list.

Able to choose if you want to receive Instant Messages (blocking IM from everyone or anyone not on your select "friends" list).

Risks

Same as nonmember above who is just visiting MySpace.com but with added risks of …

Now being able to search for and find inappropriate content, join groups, visit forums, or access blogs, any of which might contain disturbing content you deem inappropriate for your teen to see or hear.

Able to create content that could be negative in terms of image, perception by "friends," or impact on friends who have access to your teen's profile.

Able to communicate with any other MySpace member who has a profile set to public.

Where Do You Draw the Line for Your Teen?

Regarding: Registering as a MySpace member, but keeping profile set to private and limiting friends to people already known and approved of by parents.

Yes, you can if Mom or Dad is on "friends" list.	Yes, you can with these restrictions.	I'm thinking about it.	Not yet.

Draw the line somewhere on the continuum above for your teen at this time

Level Three

Registering as a MySpace member, known "friends" only, choosing degree of openness by using account settings for your profile, blog, IM, and other content areas set at least to "friends only." These choices graduate from: (1) private; (2) known friends only with friends screened carefully by parent and parent as one of friends; (3) known friends only with friends screened carefully by parent but parent not mandatory as "friend"; (4) known friends only with friends screened carefully by teen using parental guidelines and parents checking to make sure good choices are being made; (5) known friends only with friends screened carefully by teen with discretion, less parental monitoring.

Rewards

Teen can connect with a community of friends with the multimedia tools made available free by MySpace. This provides a chance to develop closer relationships with a select group of "friends," opportunity to develop discernment and friendship skills, while parents are monitoring without bringing attention to themselves. This provides better opportunity to see areas where your teen may need to develop interpersonal skills or areas related to values that you want to discuss further with your teen.

Risks

Registering as a MySpace member and creating a personal profile puts content you create "out there" for someone to see. The risks graduate based on whom your teen allows access to the profile and content. Risks also graduate based on the kind of image your teen projects and what is communicated.

Where Do You Draw the Line for Your Teen?

Regarding: registering as a MySpace member, known "friends" only, choosing degree of openness by using account settings for your profile, blog, IM, and other content areas set at least to "friends only." .

```
———————————|—————————|—————————|—————————|—————————|———————————
         (1)        (2)        (3)        (4)        (5)
```

Draw a line somewhere on the continuum above for your teen at this time. Look for the description of the numbers in the first paragraph of "Level Three."

Level Four

Moving from (1) only "friends" known to you in real life, (2) to adding "friends" to your MySpace list who are not known to you in real life, (3) to adjusting account settings and privacy settings for content and contacts to be less private and more open all the way, (4) to being public (these include profile page, blogs, IM).

Rewards

There are reasons people may choose to take on greater risks in order to include people unknown in real life and to set profile to public. Some common reasons include that they want to be able to be found by long-lost friends or relatives looking for their profile, or they are trying to promote their creative content and need to be public to do so.

Risks

Risks increase significantly whenever your teen goes from allowing only friends known in real life to allow someone unknown in real life to be added to their "friends" list. By giving unknown persons access to your profile even if it is set to friends only, your content and life is open to someone who may not be what they seem. One could forget who is among their friends and send out a bulletin or event notice giving unknown persons access to your teen in real life.

All depends on whether that personally unknown "friend" is trustworthy or a deceiver with dangerous motives and aims. Risks increase progressively as a MySpace user moves settings from "private" to "friends only" to "public." If your teen is trying to convince you to let him make the leap to friends unknown in real life and going "public," make sure you weigh the risks carefully and discuss the dangers before making this leap.

Where Do You Draw the Line for Your Teen?

(1)	(2)	(3)	(4)
Known friends settings "private" or "friends" only	Some unknown friends settings "friends" only	Account settings less "private"	Account settings set to public

Draw the line somewhere on the continuum above for your teen at this time. Look at the description of the numbers in the first paragraph of "Level Four."

Level Five

Beware! You are going into the danger zone! (1) Having profile set to public and including unknown "friends"; (2) creating content that sends out a message that is sexually inviting and/or provocative (not just sexually provocative but also provoking anger by making controversial statements); (3) being indiscrete, sharing personal information that would let someone find *where* you are and/or *when* you are going to be there; (4) using MySpace to seek out dangerous sexual encounters or other dangerous meetings (like setting up a fight); and (5) crossing the line into illegal activities that MySpace will report to law enforcement if discovered.

Rewards

I see no rewards to this progression of behavior that are worth the risks. If you discover your teen is behaving in this way, intervene and get help immediately (some of the referrals on pages 211–213 will help you make a start).

Risks

If your teen is using MySpace this way, he or she is inviting danger, perhaps sexual or physical assault! Good thing you are reading this book and will be able to discover this and take action to deal with the problems and serious risks.

Where Do You Draw the Line for Your Teen?

If your teen has ventured into these high-risk areas, the question becomes less of *where* to draw the line and more of *how* you draw the line and enforce it. The choices for intervention include: personal confrontation, removing the profile, reporting it to MySpace and they will remove it, seeking professional counseling, or even — in cases where you discover someone is in danger from your teen or your teen is in danger — contacting law enforcement.

Where is your teen on this progression? (Hopefully nowhere!) Look at the description of the numbers in the first paragraph of "Level Five."

(1)	*(2)*	*(3)*	*(4)*	*(5)*

If you discover that your teen has entered into this danger zone, what do you think would be best to do? In what order?

> *Confront your teen and give consequences for the behavior.*
> *Have teen remove profile.*
> *Report to MySpace and have them remove it (with or without telling your teen).*
> *Seek professional counseling.*
> *Contact law enforcement.*

Hopefully, most parents will not have to confront such decisions, but parents do their teen and society a service by not turning a blind eye.

You Decide Where to Draw the Line for Your Teen

Keeping in mind all that you have learned in this book, consider the rewards versus the risks for your teen at this point in his or her maturing process. Then literally draw the line where you deem it best for your teen. If you decide that MySpace is not rewarding enough for your teen to warrant the risks, make that decision, but now you can make it with confidence — even if your teen weeps or howls or reacts however dramatically.

When to Forbid MySpace Use

While in general I don't think it's a good idea to ban MySpace outright, there are instances where such a ban (or at the least severe restrictions) might be warranted. When is it recommended to ban MySpace use?

- Any time your teen is not operating safely. You gain a fair assessment of this as you work through this book with your teen. You may conclude that MySpace is not safe for any teen and decide to direct your teen to other alternative social networking sites or to other means of communication.
- Any time your teen is under the age of fourteen, which is the age they must *say* that they are to get a MySpace profile.
- Any time your teen violates the Terms of Use set by MySpace.
- Any time your teen refuses to abide by the agreements you require in order to begin using MySpace. For example, you may require that you be listed as a "friend" so you can monitor your teen's profile for awhile until you are sure he is operating safely. If your teen refuses to agree to this, you can decide not to allow MySpace use.

If your teen is already using MySpace and you want to make sure she stays safe, you can make continued use contingent on making changes to stay safe and conform to whatever standards you as the parent in authority set. It's best to lay out clearly the required standards (which you can do in the section on "Where Do You Draw the Line for Your Teen"). Then lay out the progressive consequences for violations.

Start your teens out on green. If there is an infraction, they get their first warning and are on "yellow" — sort of like getting a yellow card in soccer. If there is a second infraction, they are on "red," which means that if they step outside the parameters you set one more time, you will delete their MySpace page. This progressive warning system will make sure that they have time to mend their ways before suffering the loss of their MySpace network.

Deleting a Teen's MySpace Page

If you decide that the drastic step of deleting a MySpace page is warranted, be prepared for an extreme emotional reaction. We need to accept that when we tell our teen to delete their MySpace page, it's different from telling them to hang up the phone or stay away from strangers. To them deleting their MySpace page is more like telling them to throw their artwork into the fire or to delete *themselves*. It's telling them to disconnect from their circle of friends, invite ridicule, and throw out their calendar and all their notes from their friends while they are at it. It probably feels something like burning letters and bridges, because once a MySpace account is deleted, those connections, messages, comments, and kudos *cannot be retrieved*.

Deleting your teen's MySpace account also carries with it a lot of peer pressure and potential embarrassment, because if they are not allowed on MySpace and most of their friends are, their friends who remain will be keenly aware of their absence.

We make this restriction the same way a caring parent makes any other difficult decision that is best for our child. It may be helpful to think in terms similar to explaining why a young child needed to get a vaccination that was painful at that moment but deemed necessary for their overall safety and well-being. If we have set up the progressive warning system described above, the removal of the profile will not come as a surprise and will be the result of a choice the teen made to continue to disobey clearly set parameters. The issues will have already been discussed, if you've talked through the discussions in this book.

Thus, it will be a matter of resolve on your part to follow through on the decisions you have made for the good of your teen. Given this kind of prelude, you will be able to make the hard decision, and even comfort your teen in their grief over losing this important connection in their lives. You can also then talk about what it will require to earn this privilege again and regain your trust. You may assume that your teen will be tempted to go behind your back to get a MySpace profile in another name or one hidden from you. In advance, let your teen know what the consequences will be for doing so, and let him know that you have your ways of checking. Then follow through with those consequences if you must.

Deleting your child's MySpace profile is simple. Go to *www. MySpace.com* by typing that into the address line of your web browser. Go to the bottom of that page and click on Safety Tips. Once there, click on Tips for Parents. There will be a hyperlink on that page to allow you to delete your child's MySpace profile. Follow the instructions.

You can also find this information in the Frequently Asked Questions page, which is also accessible from the bottom of the MySpace. com home page. Before you delete your teen's MySpace page, bear in mind that there is *no way* to retrieve it. If you later agree to allow your teen to have another page, he will have to rebuild his profile, redesign the page, and try to reconnect with the people who were previously on the "friends" list.

Giving Trustworthy Teens Their Space on MySpace

While some teens need more limits, other teens by their behavior and maturity level have earned more freedom. Initially, upon your discovery of MySpace and social networking, you may have to make a careful inspection of your teen's content and involvement. However, once you set acceptable guidelines and limitations that will keep your teen safe and he complies, it's time to step back a bit.

Teens need to individuate, to develop their identity separate from Mom and Dad. We parents can keep an eye on our teens and make sure they are okay without all their "friends" knowing we're in the virtual room. Metaphorically speaking, it's the difference between your teenage daughter having a slumber party and you putting on your pajamas, popping some popcorn, and plopping yourself down on the sofa with her friends or staying upstairs, but listening to make sure all is well and peeking in on them without being seen, unless you're bringing cookies (of the noncomputer kind!).

How Not to Invade Your Teen's Space on MySpace

When communicating with your teen on MySpace, don't leave comments on their profile page. Remember, that's like posting it on the bulletin board outside a dorm room where anyone passing by can read it. Rather, send them a message or email (that is like a private note) that won't show up on their profile page for all their "friends" to see.

I learned this from my own ignorance as I was learning to communicate with my teens on MySpace. Taylor had to "talk to me" about it. After a performance of his—which was truly wonderful, although I'm a bit partial—I sent him a message. At least *I thought* I was sending him a *message* when I was actually sending him a *comment*. That showed up among his "friends" photos and comments on his profile page for all to see. He made me promise in this book to tell all the other parents not to do this on their teen's page. No matter how much they love us, any self-respecting seventeen-year-old would find something like that embarrassing. He deleted it immediately and let me know why. It looked like this:

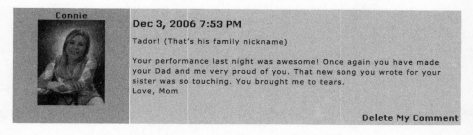

> **Connie**
>
> **Dec 3, 2006 7:53 PM**
>
> Tador! (That's his family nickname)
>
> Your performance last night was awesome! Once again you have made your Dad and me very proud of you. That new song you wrote for your sister was so touching. You brought me to tears.
> Love, Mom
>
> **Delete My Comment**

Bottom line: Don't leave embarrassing comments on your teen's page; send a message instead. Let their personal profile be an expression of their identity as an individual without being overshadowed.

◄◄ ►►

You are the chief security officer for your teen. Get the support of your group (if you've formed one) or your spouse, and draw the line. You may want to articulate to your teen the factors that went into your decision, which you should be better able to do now. You may want to set a date to reconsider your lines based on your teen's demonstrated growth in maturity.

If you draw the line somewhere that allows MySpace use, you are invited to come to "My Space" at *www.myspace.com/momsanddads*, where we can learn together how to use MySpace for our teen's good. You're welcome to join in even if you decide not to let your teen do so for now. If your teen prefers Xanga, you can go to *www.xanga.com/dadsandmoms*. If your teen prefers a Christian MySpace alternative, check out *www.xianz.com/momsanddads*. I hope to meet you there!

A Safety Checklist for Busy Parents

You've familiarized yourself with MySpace. You've recognized that you are the most important person in the room in terms of monitoring your teen's safety, and you've learned some of the commonsense advice for staying safe. Finally, you've thought about your teen's development and maturity level, and you've decided to allow him to use MySpace within certain boundaries. Now let's look quickly at the concrete ways you can set and enforce safety checks, based on your understanding of your teen's maturity.

For those times when you're too busy for an in-depth perusal of your teen's MySpace experience, or if you are too busy to learn to navigate MySpace on your own but not too busy to make sure your teen is safe, I've created this MySpace safety checklist. Think of it as similar to a pocket voters' guide, a checklist of what you need to look for and key areas of your teen's MySpace profile you need to examine to make sure your teen stays safe. By giving periodic checks, you will be able to keep him or her in line with the account settings and guidelines you have decided on or agreed on with your teen.

On some of these items, you may need to ask your teen to show you and help you look. If your teen says she doesn't know how to do these things, then she doesn't have the skills to navigate MySpace safely and should not be allowed to do so. Don't forget that you are the parent; it is reasonable to make using MySpace contingent on keeping everything in line with what you deem safe and good. Think of it as driver's training for getting around safely in a social networking site. The checks can be at set intervals (weekly or every other week), or you can keep it unsystematic to add an element of surprise.

Remember, this is not a game of Gotcha! Your aim should be to help your teen develop the skills and good judgment to get to the point where he no longer *needs* you to be checking up on him. Your attitude will make a big difference in whether this is a productive exercise. If these checkups are done with a positive attitude, affirming all that your teen is doing right and calmly discussing anything that may need to be adjusted for the sake of safety, these can be pleasant times of interaction. If you go in looking only for what is wrong, picking apart their content, and acting like a censor for *Pravda*, these checkups may end up being unpleasant and unproductive.

Be respectful and tread lightly when you are looking at the content of any page. Be careful not to crush your teen's spirit with nit-picky editing. They are not looking for an English teacher with a red pen. They simply want to be able to stay on their favorite social networking site and communicate with their friends. Your aim should be to make sure they are staying safe, not to make sure they are saying the things you would say or posting the photos you would post. That's what *your* MySpace profile is for and why it's called *My*Space. This is personal, so be as respectful and positive as you can be.

To make this work well, we parents need to think of ourselves as teaming up with our teens to help them progress to protecting themselves online. We probably approach this with many fears. Our interactions with them will go better if we own up to our fears. Perhaps say something like this to your teen: "It's not that I distrust you, I just need to be assured you're safe. I'm afraid, and I need your help to overcome my fears by seeing that you are using good judgment. The sooner you help me see that you are operating safely, the sooner I can loosen up." Try not to come off like the internet police. Be who you are—a loving parent concerned for your teen's well-being.

We must also bear in mind how long our teens have been using a social networking site, what their age is, and how close they are to being adults. With older teens who are almost adults we must allow for more of their personal choices and accept that their personal tastes may not be our tastes. Maybe you don't like their choice of music for their page. Pick your battles. Is that a hill you're ready to die on to get your teen to change now when in a few months' time he will be an adult? We have to distinguish between safety issues and style choices that are a matter of self-expression.

Remember, you are being allowed into the inner life of your teen and his network of friends. Even though it's being shared on MySpace, it's being shared selectively. At times you may be allowed a glimpse into their private world and you can see their friends as they are trying to figure out who they are. Step carefully or you won't be welcomed in again. Of course, if you meet with resistance and your teen refuses to let you see their page, you may have to play the parent card. But generally speaking, the more you show respect and are willing to listen to your teen's explanations, he or she won't feel the need to hide from you.

As you progress along these lines, the time will come when you won't need to do these safety checks or to worry about your teen's social networking interactions. You will be rightfully assured that your teens have the skills and motivation to keep themselves safe online. Let's hope that's before they move away from home!

Safety Checklist for Busy Parents

Where's the Computer?

The computer your teen uses for social networking is best situated in the most highly trafficked room of your home. If your teen is using a laptop or other portable mode of accessing MySpace, you need to know where that is and keep it in as public a place as possible.

The thought that Mom or someone else passing by might see something objectionable is strong motivation for a teen not to go to certain places. Behind closed doors the temptations may seem impossible to resist — and not just on MySpace; indeed, MySpace is mild compared to much of what is available on the internet. Therefore, if your family uses a portable computer to access the internet, one safety rule dictates is that it be used only in a public part of the home.

Check the Account Settings

The fundamental way to make MySpace as safe as can be is to set the account settings toward greater privacy. The settings given below are as safe as can be. You can lessen the restrictions as your teen grows in maturity and requests greater freedom. Your teen will explain the reasons when the time comes to consider loosening the restrictions. You decide if and when to make those adjustments.

Thomas Jefferson said, "The price of freedom is eternal vigilance." As we allow our teens greater freedom, we also need to exercise vigilance in monitoring the degree to which they are ready to handle the freedom responsibly. So let's look at account settings designed to keep users as safe as can be. If the answer doesn't directly impact safety, I've left that decision open for you to decide.

Your part of the script for the conversation with your teen is in bold:

Mom or Dad say this: **Please take me to your Privacy Settings**.

To get there you go to your teen's MySpace personal home page; click on Account Settings to the right of the default photo under the "Hello!" greeting. You should see a list like this of account settings listed. Out of those your teen will select the privacy setting, and you will see something like this. Note the checks selected. These are the safest:

If your teen wants to give you reasons that these restrictions may be unnecessary and too much of a hassle, consider that. For example, "Comments: approve before posting" may not be necessary if their "friends" are not prone to leaving anything but good comments. It's a hassle to have to approve every comment and the other person gets a notice that their comment has to be screened. That can be taken to mean that your teen doesn't trust his friends. So your teen might be able to convince you with good evidence that this restriction is not needed given his friends. This can be backed up by showing you their comments and by your seeing that they are okay.

Who Can View My Full Profile
⦿ My Friends Only
○ Public

Privacy Settings
☑ Friend Requests - Require email or last name
☑ Comments - approve before posting
☑ Hide Online Now
☑ Show My Birthday to my Friends
☑ Photos - No Forwarding
☑ Blog Comments - Friends Only
☑ Friend Requests - No Bands

Group Invite Privacy Settings
Block Group Invites From:
☐ Everyone (including my friends)
☑ Users who are not added to my friends
☑ Bands (who are not added to my friends)
☑ Filmmakers (who are not added to my friends)
☑ Comedians (who are not added to my friends)

Event Invite Privacy Settings
Block Event Invites From:
☐ Everyone (including my friends)
☑ Users who are not added to my friends
☑ Bands (who are not added to my friends)
☑ Filmmakers (who are not added to my friends)
☑ Comedians (who are not added to my friends)

[Change Settings] [Cancel]

Mom or Dad say this: **Please take me to your IM Privacy Settings.**

The safest setting is "No one can IM me."

The next safest setting is "Only friends can IM me."

However, IM is a helpful feature if used judiciously and if the "friends" list is limited to trusted friends. Discuss this with your teen and choose between "No one can IM me" or "Only friends can IM me."

Mom or Dad say this: **Please take me to your Calendar Settings.**

To get there you would go to your teen's MySpace personal home page; click on Account Settings to right of the default photo under the "Hello!" greeting. You should see a list of account settings. Out of those your teen will select the calendar setting.

You are looking for the Calendar Sharing box. From the drop-down list your teen should choose between "Disabled" or "Share with Friends."

The safest setting is "Disabled," which makes your calendar private.

The next safest setting is "Share with Friends."

If your teen has "Share with Everyone" selected, that makes their calendar open to all, making them vulnerable.

Mom or Dad say this: **Please take me to your Profile Settings.**

Look to make sure that "Display groups I belong to" is *not* checked. The people in the groups already know he belongs. Displaying groups can open doors for predators to reach a teen more easily.

◄◄ ►►

That covers all the *safety related* items under Account Settings; the rest are basically preferences for how your teen wants to use MySpace. Moving on ...

Mom or Dad say this: **Please take me to your My Friends Space.**

To get there you would go to your teen's MySpace personal home page, scroll down and look for "My Friends Space," with thumbnails of top friends showing; click on "View All of My Friends."

Look at Profile and User Names of current friends:

Look for: Friends known in real life and approved of by parents.

Treat this virtual friend check the way you would whenever your teen brings home a new friend. Ask whatever questions you need to ask. If your teen has a great group of friends, thank God, and let your teen know how pleased you are with his choice of friends. If someone has slipped in who is unknown or does not meet agreed-upon criteria, it may be time to discuss who is or is not a friend. It is possible to delete anyone from the "friends" list. But before you do, you need to hear the defense of a friend you may doubt. I found out that one of my teen's friends had the F*** word on his profile page. So I asked about him. When I heard his life story, I understood why he might use such foul language and why my teen overlooked that language in an attempt to reach out and try to make his life better. Also, remind your teen to check their "friends" list before sending bulletins or event invitations.

Mom or Dad say this: **Please take me to your Pics.**
(Repeat process for Videos.)

The pics link is located on your teen's MySpace personal home page, directly under the default photo and "Hello" greeting (videos are right next to it).

Look for any information in the photos that could give away location, embarrass someone, is a copyright infringement, or anything you deem inappropriate.

Read captions to make sure private information isn't given away there.

If you like the photos they've chosen or the content of what's being done in the photos, be sure to voice your approval.

Mom or Dad say this: **Please take me to your Profile Home Page.**

Experience their page. Listen to their music, look at their creative self-expression, read what has been posted, check the details and comments. Ask them to make whatever changes you deem necessary for the sake of safety or reputation.

Music: Ask to listen to the music they have chosen to play. Listen to the lyrics as well as the musical style.

Read over: Interests, Music, Movies, Television, Books, Heroes (Kudos to you if you made that list!), About Me, Who I'd Like to Meet. Discuss anything you share in common (like favorites). Commend everything you find to commend. If you find anything you deem unsafe, have teen correct it to your satisfaction.

Details: Read over Details. If, like our family, you don't go for horoscopes, understand that to date there is no way to remove the zodiac sign from the details section. Your teen didn't actively choose this. It is put in automatically based on the birth date submitted during registration. If you want birthday greetings, you have to accept the zodiac sign in the deal.

Comments: Skim over the contents of the comments. Your teen cannot, of course, control the kind of comments someone else makes. But he can control what to do with them. The choices available include:

Your teen can check comments before posting.

Your teen can delete inappropriate comments.

Your teen can delete a person from the "friends" list.

Your teen can block a user and then delete from "friends" list.

Mom or Dad say this: **Please take me to the Bulletins you have posted.**

To get there you would go to your teen's MySpace personal home page (the one that precedes the profile page), scroll down, and look for My Bulletin Space, with thumbnails showing bulletins *received*, click on View All Bulletin Entries under list of bulletins. Don't look at the list of bulletins *sent to* your teen. Your teen probably doesn't read all bulletins received anyway and cannot be held liable for what is posted by others. You want to see the bulletins *sent by* your teen. To do so your teen would click on Show Bulletins I've Posted.

Look at the bulletins posted *by* your teen. Look for personal information like phone number, dates, times, and locations of events or meetings. Teens sometimes forget and put such detail in the bulletins to their friends. Have them delete any information that makes them vulnerable.

Your basic MySpace quick safety check is complete! Congratulations! You can rest easier, knowing that your teen is learning how to stay safe on MySpace.

MySpace for Families of Faith

Ashley's dad is a pastor who's also an involved parent. He went through the process of exploring MySpace with her and came to the decision that the risks were not worth the rewards. I commend him for taking the time and effort to explore social networking and trust that he knows what is best for his teenage daughter. Thankfully, Ashley is respectful of her dad's decision.

Many families of faith have shied away from MySpace because of various concerns. At a conference for the Internet Evangelism Coalition, I heard a variety of reasons given. If MySpace really is a predator's playground, why would I even consider letting my teen go there? Why allow your teens to be bombarded further by the world if you don't have to? One Christian leader of a media organization said, "I would use MySpace for outreach with the gospel, but I certainly would not recommend that parents let their teens go there."

Other parents at this conference allowed their teens to go on MySpace in order to mentor them in the best way to be in the world but not of the world.

Each parent is responsible to make those decisions; for my part, I will supply information of options available to families of faith who decide either to allow or disallow MySpace.

Christian MySpace Alternatives

For those who decide to avoid MySpace because they want their teens to experience social networking in a more sheltered and Christian network, there are numerous Christian MySpace alternatives that serve the same basic functions as MySpace and other social networking sites but with a Christian focus, Christian groups, and more rigorous screening of content. This is an emerging field, so I'm sure the players will change and popularity will wax and wane from site to site. The best way to get up-to-date listings of Christian social networking sites is to conduct a search using a computer search engine (like Yahoo! or Google or Answers.com). Type in "Christian MySpace" or "Christian Social Networking Site" and see what comes up.

The Christian alternative social networking sites you might try are:

- *www.Xianz.com*
- *www.MyPraize.com*
- *www.boc.org (boc = Body of Christ)*
- *www.meetfish.com (sponsored by the American Tract Society)*
- *www.Holypal.com*
- *www.DittyTalk.com*
- *www.yourChristianspace.com*
- *www.jcfaith.com*
- *www.ChristUnion.com*
- *www.Biblelounge.com*
- *www.Christianblog.com*
- *www.ChristianTeenForums.com* (This one is a hybrid. Over 5,000 Christian teens are connected at this website, but they are also a group on MySpace at *http://groups.myspace.com/ctfgroup*)

Each of the Christian MySpace alternative sites are a little different from each other and from MySpace, but they basically serve the same functions. You will notice variations in technological sophistication and formats. For example, Body of Christ Online (*www.boc.com*) is geared more toward allowing church groups to continue their fellowship online, and their format reflects this. Xianz has a look and feel very much like MySpace, but the ads are for Christian colleges, Christian books, independent Christian rock, and such.

A *USA Today* online blog, entitled *Generation Next*, addressed this new development in online social networking in an article titled *A Christian MySpace?* It stated:

In the rather niche world of Christian television programming, teens can choose to watch Christian reality shows and Christ-inspired animation or Christian hip-hop and rock music videos. So it was only logical that the wildly popular framework of personal profiles and user-generated content would be brought into the fold. On BattleCry.com, a site sponsored by Teen Mania, teens are "working together to save a generation." How? By building personal profiles, networking online and blogging about their battles to convert the "unchurched" and avoid corrosive music and media.[1]

So, if your family has decided that you prefer not to have your teen develop online relationships through MySpace, you can check out the Christian alternatives. Indeed, as the blog points out, there are "Christian alternatives" to most of what the world has to offer.

Nevertheless, it is important that you not let your sense of safety in allowing your child to join a Christian site cause you or your teen to let down your guard. Everything we have covered in this book should be considered within the context of whatever social networking site your teen uses. The belief that one is in a "safe, Christian environment" can create a false sense of security. Consider this comment posted after the *USA Today: Generation Next* blog. One teenage reader wrote:

> Battle Cry is so awesome. You can talk to people without having to worry if they're perverts or not. You can talk to other Christian people about your battles and other cool things that are happening to you. I think it's the best way to get teenagers to stop talking to perverts.[2]

Do you see the problem here? What is to stop a so-called "pervert" from seeing a Christian social networking site as a better place to go looking for his next prey? Trust is central to the way sexual predators lure and groom their victims. So if a predator is devious enough to go to a Christian social networking site, he may have a head start toward getting the trust needed to make the next move. If he knows enough Christian jargon and buzz words, he's in.

If parents aren't overseeing what their teen is doing because they feel safer with a Christian site, the danger increases. Suppose the said predator hangs out on the site and the teens become comfortable enough with each other to share about their church youth groups. It's only a click away to the church website and possibly a calendar of youth group events where those teens "sharing" online will be in person. What's to stop an aggressive predator from going to the skating rink and "happening to run in to" the teen he's become attracted to and gotten to know via the Christian site? What's to stop him from going further and volunteering to work with the youth group?

I don't mean to scare you further, but this is a valid fear. But it is fear that can be managed. If you have gone through this book and adapt the safety measures I've applied to MySpace to whatever social networking site your teen is using and remain an involved parent, you can teach your teen to develop the security sense required for interacting online in this day and age of technological wonders. This might also be a good time to call your youth pastor and check on how he or she goes about screening details on the church's website and youth ministry volunteers. Since the technology has changed, our security precautions in the local church need to change too.

This kind of danger isn't new; only the technology is new. Jesus himself warned us: "Watch out for false prophets. They come to you in sheep's clothing, but inwardly they are ferocious wolves" (Matthew 7:15). Why should we be surprised that wolves in sheep's clothing would be lurking on Christian social networking sites, especially when the increased security precautions and collaboration with law enforcement make MySpace less appealing to predators? So we must deal with the danger and teach our teens that heaven is the place where righteousness dwells; here on earth we need to maintain a healthy dose of skepticism and cautious self-protection.

This is not to say that a Christian alternative site would not be good for your teen. In response to the *USA Today: Generation Next* blog, one youth pastor replied:

> I am a member of Battle Cry and this Website is one of the best things our youth group has come across in a long time! I see all my kids so excited and communicating amongst Christian friends and praying with and for each other. This is awesome! It is also great to know they don't have to see these inappropriate ads on their screen every time they go to log on to MySpace. Praise God for Battle Cry![3]

Objections You May Encounter

Again, this is a matter of your weighing the rewards and risks, discussing things with your teen, and deciding what is best for your family.

There are a few considerations you may run into, however, if you decide to insist your teen use a Christian MySpace alternative.

"None of my friends are there."

This complaint may be valid. The numbers of users on a Christian alternative site is miniscule compared to the multitudes on MySpace. If they go to a public school and all their classmates who use social networking are on MySpace, Facebook, or Xanga, the alternative of going to a Christian site will disconnect them from their peers—which you may see as a good thing, but they may not.

Think of it as if all their friends were going to a popular skating rink or fast food place, but you suggest that they go to another one where few if any of their friends will be. True, they could do the same things, but it's not the same. Teens don't go skating just for exercise or go out for fast food just for nourishment. Whether they want to go depends on who is going to be there. Social networking is mainly about the social network. So unless your teen has a group of friends to migrate with her to the Christian alternative site, this may be a hard sell.

"It's lame."

This probably means the site doesn't work properly, is slow, or breaks down a lot. One of the reasons MySpace became so popular compared to other sites was because they made the technology easy to use and fix it promptly when it goes down. If the site your teen is trying to use doesn't work well, the Christian environment will lose its luster.

"It's fake."

Translated, this means that with the screening and lack of acceptance for certain words, beliefs, and so on, it loses the authenticity that seemingly makes MySpace attractive.

Your teen may say, "That is for Christians who aren't bold enough to be in the world but not of the world." If your teen says this, you may have an evangelist or missionary on your hands. That's good! If they are called to go into all the world and preach the gospel, MySpace may be the best place for that.

In the following excerpt from the book *Web-Empower Your Church: Unleashing the Power of Internet Ministry* by Mark Stephenson, note what he is looking for in the perfect mission field:

> If we were going to design the perfect mission field, here is what it might look like:
>
> 1. It would be filled with millions of unsaved and accessible youth and young adults.
> 2. It would be a place where people openly, regularly, and publicly share their opinions, thoughts, feelings, concerns, fears, and needs without anyone asking them to.
> 3. It would be a place where people connect with other people in community, and people like and expect to meet new people.
> 4. It would be a place where many people provide a picture and a little information about themselves so you can know a little about them before you communicate with them.
> 5. It would be a place where it is okay to be creative, different, and to just be you.
> 6. It would be a place where people openly debate, discuss, and exchange ideas including spiritual matters.
> 7. It would be a place where people like to go and hang out. It would be fun, sometimes silly, and people would smile and laugh.
> 8. It would be a place that is very close to our home so we could get there quickly when we have some time, and getting there would not require immunizations, or passports, or plane trips. And it would all be free.
>
> This perfect mission field exists right now, down to the last detail. It exists on the Internet in public online services that connect people in community: blogs, personal web pages, and discussion groups, including social networking sites such as MySpace.com.[4]

So, for families of faith, we must consider what our teens are using MySpace or a Christian social networking site *for* before we make our decisions. We may end up deciding that they will use both for different reasons. They can use MySpace or Christian sites to access Christian media and bands. Several well-known ministry leaders and ministries have a MySpace page, including Joyce Meyer, Tony Campolo, many churches, and Campus Crusade for Christ (www.myspace.com/

agapespace); other ministries are joining. So they could look there and observe how these ministries present themselves and the gospel to the world. Your teen's youth group could train up MySpace missionaries, going into discussion forums about faith and Christianity with older teens and a parent or mentor to help them encounter the questions being asked about faith and together devising answers. Here, we have to use our creativity as the technology and various sites develop.

There are so many amazing and wonderful ways faith communities and church youth ministries could use MySpace or Christian MySpace alternatives that it boggles the mind. Families of any faith have the option of redeeming the use of MySpace to enhance their family's spiritual development. Also note that content like videos and music is available free to download to your site. Christian Broadcasting Network and *The 700 Club* plan to make a library of video clips available free to anyone who wants to use them to enhance their personal profile and use them to help spread the good news of God's love. So check with the ministries you enjoy to see if your teen can use their content on their page and in that way share God's love with their friends.

Using MySpace to Make a Difference in Real-Life Missions

Not only can our teens contact ministries through MySpace, they can use MySpace to make a positive difference in the real world. They can do things to impact their world using their MySpace page.

My daughter Haley began to have an interest in mission work through her church youth group. She went to Mexico to build houses. Back home, she put up a photo travel blog on her MySpace page to share her memories and photos with friends and family.

She felt called to go to Africa on a mission trip. When such a trip was announced at her church, she had to raise $3,000 to participate. She set to work raising money by working, but she also asked for donations. We found out that we could use her MySpace page and PayPal account to receive donations online that would go directly to the church so donors could track them and get a tax deduction without her having to handle the money or keep an accounting.

So Haley set up a secondary MySpace page that focused on her mission work, specifically the Africa trip, and displayed photos from past mission trips. I wrote a donor request letter that we sent to family and friends where we included the URL address to her MySpace mission's page (*www.myspace.com/haleyfacemissions*). As I write this, Haley is in Nigeria showing *The Jesus Film* to the Zing people, a population of about 300,000, of whom roughly half have never been reached with the gospel.

Now as I edit this, Haley has returned from her trip and has posted photos and slide shows from her trip. She plans to add a blog/travel diary to share the experience with those who made it possible for her to go through their donations, prayer, and support. While Haley was gone, I discovered another benefit to her MySpace missions page. During her time in Nigeria, a Nigerian airplane crashed and almost one hundred people died. I was able to send a bulletin to the friends on her missions page to let them know Haley's team was not on that flight (and to ask them to pray for the loved ones of those who died).

In this way and many others I'm sure I haven't thought of yet, teens can find their place in the larger world and actually reach out and make a difference, using the technological wonders of MySpace and the internet.

Overcoming Evil with Good

God chose us and our teens to be alive in this exciting age of online social networking. Do we really want to bury this treasure in the ground just because we are afraid? The man in the parable of the talents who took what he was given to invest but did nothing with it out of fear was reprimanded severely by the Lord. Scripture tells us, "Do not be overcome by evil, but overcome evil with good" (Romans 12:21).

So while making sure our teens are not being stained by the world's wickedness, we should also make sure we're not neglecting the positive possibilities. There are many ways we can use MySpace and similar Christian sites for sharing our faith or engaging in Christian fellowship. We have to decide whether we want our teens to use such sites as a monastery or a mission field, and both are variously appropriate. We dare not neglect the wonders of technology just because we are afraid or uninformed. I trust that you will not, because you are reading this book and showing active interest in this area of your teen's life. Good for you; better for your teen!

Epilogue

I commend you for making it all the way through this book! I'm sure your relationship with your teen or teens will be better for it. I tried to make sure I would help you learn what you need to know to make your own decision for the good of your family regarding the use of MySpace and social networking sites like it. I trust that you have done so.

Now that the book is coming to its close and you have already decided where to draw the line for your family, I want to add some comments about the positive possibilities I've discovered in my MySpace relationship with my teens and their friends.

When I was a youth pastor, one of the greatest challenges was to help parents get a feel for the real world and youth culture in which their teens lived. We showed videos that took parents through a day behind the eyes of an ordinary teen, seeing what they saw, hearing what they heard, and feeling the pressures they felt at home, at school, at work, and in their social circles. This was okay as far as it went, but that "ordinary" teen was not *my* teen, nor was it *your* teen.

Today, much of the teen world is wrapped up in social networking sites like MySpace. Even if you choose not to allow your teen to go on MySpace, I urge you to create a profile and get to know your teen's real world through this virtual window. When you see the kinds of issues their friends are struggling with and hear the kind of comments going back and forth between their friends, you will know better how to guide, how to encourage, and how to pray.

Here are a few ways a parent can use MySpace positively on behalf of their teen, even if you choose not to allow your teen on a social networking site for now:

- Get to know what's happening in your teen's school and social circles.
- Discover what music is influencing your teen's friends.
- View how your teen's friends represent themselves to the world (an excellent resource to check before allowing a sleepover).
- Find out where your teen is when you need to reach him or her immediately (you can send a bulletin to or through one of their friends to check with all of their friends to see if anyone knows where they are).
- Keep your family calendar organized by incorporating the items on your teen's MySpace calendar into your family calendar or keep your family calendar on MySpace (just set it to private).
- Support their positive interests.

If you choose to start an interactive online relationship with your teen, prepare for a deeper level of relationship. I cannot adequately measure the value of what I have learned about the inner life of my teens, their concerns, their joys, their jokes, and their thoughts through MySpace. We have somehow connected on another level. There is something about writing to each other, reading each other's blogs, viewing the pics, and commenting on them that has deepened and enriched our connection. This, to me, was a big part of what persuaded me to allow them progressive levels of freedom to use MySpace.

I know that each one of us will consider and reconsider these kinds of questions regarding the quickly changing technologies that are revolutionizing our teen's world and relationships. I hope this book has helped you now and that you will put it on a shelf to go back to it as your teen grows and matures, to reconsider it in the future. I respect whatever decisions you have made and will make. No one knows your teen or loves your teen better than you do!

Remember too that you are the most powerful person in the room when it comes to protecting your teen. Whether you do that through monitoring their MySpace use, monitoring their use of a Christian MySpace alternative, monitoring their use of any other social networking site, or deciding that social networking is not right for them at this time, your involvement in this area of their lives will go a long way toward keeping them safe and helping them mature to one day deal with these issues safely on their own.

I sincerely hope this book has helped you make those decisions. I'd love to "meet you" in cyberspace at one of my social networking pages associated with this book: *www.myspace.com/momsanddads, www. Xanga.com/dadsandmoms,* or *www.Xianz.com/momsanddads.*

Notes

Chapter 1: What Is MySpace?

1. This legend from India is widely available on the internet. Simply type "Blind Men and Elephant" in the Google search box, and many renditions of it will come up.

Chapter 2: The World Has Changed

1. David Hart, *NSF Shapes the Internet's Evolution*, National Science Foundation website, *www.nsf.gov/discoveries/disc_summ.jsp?cntn_id=100662&org=NSF* (accessed Nov. 24, 2006).
2. Thomas L. Friedman, *The World Is Flat* (New York: Farrar, Straus & Giroux, 2006), 125.
3. See Dawn Kawamoto and Greg Sandoval, "MySpace Growth Continues amid Criticism." Posted March 31, 2006 on *ZDNet News*: *http://news.zdnet. com/2100-9595_22-6056580.html*
4. Rupert Murdoch, as reported by *Hollywood Reporter, Reuters*, July 25, 2006. *www.woopidoo.com/biography/rupert-murdoch/myspace.htm* (accessed October 25, 2006).

Chapter 3: Why Teens Love MySpace

1. Brenda Ueland, *If You Want to Write: A Book about Art, Independence and Spirit* (St. Paul, MN: Graywolf, 1938, 1987), 3.
2. Ibid, 4.

Chapter 5: Welcome to the MySpace Visitor's Center

1. "MySpace.com Terms of Use Agreement," *www.myspace.com/Modules/Common/ Pages/TermsConditions.aspx* (accessed October 22, 2006).

2. If you have any questions about this privacy statement, the practices of this site, or your dealings with this website, please contact us at: privacy@myspace.com (8391 Beverly Blvd, #349, Los Angeles, CA 90048).

Chapter 7: Communicating with Friends and Peers on MySpace

1. John Hoellwarth, "Corps Ask MySpace Friends to Honor Values," *Marine Corps Times, www.marinetimes.com/story.php?f=1–292925–2313141.php* (accessed October 26, 2006).

2. Atoosa Rubenstein, *Seventeen Magazine: A Guide to MySpace for Parents with Teens,* published by MySpace in association with *Seventeen Magazine* (October 2006), p. 3.

Chapter 8: Self-Expression on MySpace

1. Dr. Kathy Koch's resources, books, and DVDs, as well as contact information, are available in Appendix C.

Chapter 10: Engaging the Wider World: Forums and Chat Rooms on MySpace

1. Adapted from Connie Neal, "MySpace for Moms," *Today's Christian Woman* (January/February 2007). Used with permission.

2. *About MySpace: Safety and Security,* obtained October 18, 2006, from MySpace representative at the California Cyber-Safety Summit.

Chapter 11: Using MySpace to Fulfill Five Developmental Needs

1. Kathy Koch, *Finding Authentic Hope and Wholeness: 5 Questions That Will Change Your Life* (Chicago: Moody Press, 2005).

2. Kathy Koch, *Life-Changing Questions: Authentic Answers* (DVD) (Fort Worth, TX: Celebrate Kids Inc., 2006).

3. *www.myspace.com/invisiblechildren* (accessed October 27, 2006).

Chapter 12: Growing Your Teen's Independence Using MySpace

1. Joanne McNabb, quote given in answer to a question at California Cyber-Safety Summit on October 18, 2006, in Sacramento, California.

Chapter 13: Should *My* Teen Use MySpace?

1. See and listen for yourself at *www.myspace.com/taylornealmusic.*

Chapter 14: Basic Safety Tips for MySpace

1. "MySpace.com Safety Tips," *www.myspace.com/Modules/Common/Pages/SafetyTips.aspx* (accessed October 5, 2006).

2. "MySpace.com Safety Tips: Tips for Parents," *www.myspace.com/Modules/Common/Pages/SafetyTips.aspx* (accessed October 5, 2006).

3. Web Wise Kids, *www.wiredwithwisdom.org/our_software.asp* (accessed October 30, 2006).

4. Whitney Roban, *The Net Effect: Girls and New Media: A Report from the Girl Scout Research Institute*, p. 16, *www.girlscouts.org/research/pdf/net_effect.pdf* (accessed October 25, 2006).

5. Ibid.

6. *About MySpace Safety and Security* handout from MySpace, provided at California Cyber-Safety Summit (October 18, 2006), Sacramento.

7. Ibid.

Chapter 17: MySpace for Families of Faith

1. Venessa Mendenhall, David Andrukonis, Jeff Nelson, and Brian Wolly, "A Christian MySpace?" *USA Today: Generation Next*, *http://blogs.usatoday.com/gennext/2006/08/a_christian_mys.html* (accessed November 1, 2006).

2. Ibid., posted by: beccam (August 24, 2006, 7:54:24 P.M.).

3. Ibid., posted by Pastor Raymond Salas (August 23, 2006, 7:37:44 P.M.).

4. Mark Stephenson, *Web-Empower Your Church: Unleashing the Power of Internet Ministry* (Nashville: Abingdon, forthcoming). This quote is available at *http://ied.gospelcom.net/webmissionfield.php* ("ied" stands for Internet Evangelism Day).

Glossary of Terms

The meanings of words are changing so fast that it's hard to keep up. As I was doing research for this book, I found myself frustrated by how many words were either new to me or were used in unfamiliar ways. Since I want this book to be accessible to all who may or may not have kept up with the quickly changing terms related to computers and MySpace, I've included this glossary.

These entries are my own simple definitions based on more formal research but tailored to the parents of teens who are interested in social networking. Sometimes I will bold a word in a definition to alert you that there is a definition of that word in the glossary. I based most of these definitions on information from **answers.com**; direct quotes are in quotation marks. If my simple definitions are not sufficient or if I missed one you need, I encourage you to go to that website. There you can get a more formal definition and further help.

Answers.com. A wonderfully helpful resource for research. It is a focused collection of dictionaries, encyclopedias, almanacs, and downright useful information. This is a great help when your teens are doing research for homework! For our purposes, answers.com (found at *www.answers.com*) has another specific benefit. You can **download** a program called "1-Click." This will allow you to get instant definitions of any word or initials you don't know the meaning of in any document on your computer or any website you visit.

This program is especially helpful with some of the codes teens use to keep their communication secret from their parents, like POS (Parent Over Shoulder), LOL (Laughing Out Loud), or more dangerous ones used by predators like ASL (Age? Sex? Location?). Once you have downloaded this 1-Click program to your computer, you can press the "Alt" key on your keyboard while pointing your **cursor** at a word and simultaneously

click. A bubble will appear with the definition. With the 1-Click system you can decipher any term you need to know even though words related to new technologies are changing day by day.

Back button. When using the internet or word processing programs, there will usually be a **toolbar** across the top of the page. This may have an option that says "back"; if you **click** on this "back button," it will take you to the previous web page you visited.

Blog. Short for "weblog," a journal or log kept on a computer website. A blog "contains dated text entries in reverse chronological order (most recent first) about a particular topic. Blogs serve many purposes from **online** newsletters to personal journals to 'ranting and raving.' They can be written by one person or a group of contributors. Entries contain commentary and links to other websites, and images as well as a search facility may also be included. A blog that includes video clips is a 'video weblog.'"

Browse. "To view the contents of a file or a group of files. Browser programs generally let you view data by scrolling through the documents or databases. In a database program, the browse mode often lets you edit the data." There is a browse feature on MySpace that allows the users to browse for specific types of people by various characteristics.

Bulletin (MySpace). On MySpace a bulletin is a single message sent to everyone on your "friends" list. The title shows up on the receivers' list of bulletins and they may or may not read it. You will also receive bulletins from people on your list of MySpace friends.

Bulletin Board. See **Message board**.

Chat room. A place on a website or other internet location where people can communicate in real time by typing on their keyboard. The conversations are usually organized according to topic, often in a **forum**. "A Website or server space on the Internet where live keyboard conversations (usually organized around a specific topic) with other people occur."

Click. Most computers use a pointing device called a **mouse** that has the option of being pressed on the right or left side. When you press one of the buttons on the mouse, you hear a "click," so the word has come to stand for the action. To click usually refers to pressing on the left side of the mouse; to **right-click** is to press on the right side of the mouse, which gives you entirely different options.

Code and copying code. Code is a system of symbols that tells a computer what to do and how to do it. When MySpace users want to enhance their profile, they can go to other websites (like photobucket.com), copy code for a specific function, and put it in their MySpace profile; it will do whatever the code is designed to do. For example, to make a slide show of photos, animation, or a scrolling marquee requires a computer code.

Comment. "A statement of fact or opinion, especially a remark that expresses a personal reaction or attitude." On MySpace people can leave comments on profile pages that are public, profile pages of their friends, blogs, videos, pics, and music. Comments can also include not only text but music, pics, video, and visual images. Comments on MySpace can be deleted or limited or previewed before allowing them to be posted on your page.

Computer. "A general-purpose machine that processes data according to a set of instructions that are stored internally either temporarily or permanently. The computer and all equipment attached to it are called hardware. The instructions that tell it what to do are called 'software.' A set of instructions that perform a particular task is called a 'program' or 'software program.'"

Cookies (of the computer variety). A computer "cookie" is a data file used by some websites to track users preferences, where they go **online**, what products catch their interests, and other information. You usually don't know when cookies are in operation, but they are used—among other things—to target future advertising to the preferences of the user. These can be stored "temporarily for that session only or permanently on the hard disk (persistent cookie). Cookies provide a way for the Website to recognize you and keep track of your preferences."

Cursor. When you are using the computer, there is usually a distinct blinking line or arrow that tells you where "you" are on the screen. This is the cursor. The cursor is moved by moving your **mouse**. If you **click**, the action will take place at the point on the screen where the cursor is aimed. This is why you are told to "point and click"; you point your cursor to the place where you want something to happen and either click your mouse or type on the keyboard if you want to enter information at that point.

Cyberspace. The electronic medium in which computer interaction takes place. When you go on the internet, you are said to be in "cyberspace."

Cyber-bullying. To bully or harass someone through various means using the computer and internet communications. This can take place through such means such as text messaging, email, comments on a MySpace profile, cell phones, etc. This can include threats, unwanted communication, verbal attacks, and disseminating false or hurtful information about someone via the electronic or computer communication.

Cyber-safety. The prefix "cyber" has to do with a computer network. So cyber-safety refers to safety related to computer networks.

Default photo. On MySpace the first photo you choose to **upload** becomes your default photo. This is the photo that will show up on your profile page unless it is changed purposely.

Default setting. "A setting or value automatically assigned to a computer program or device, outside of user intervention. Such settings are also called **presets**, especially for electronic devices."

Delete. "To remove by striking out or canceling; to remove an item of data from a file or to remove a file from the disk."

Digital or digitally. Relating to a digit or something shown in numerical form or small bits of information. The small chunks of information arranged in random formation—as opposed to going in lines from left to right and top to bottom—is said to be digital. "Of or relating to a device that can read, write, or store information that is represented in numerical form."

Double-click. To click twice rapidly on the left side of your mouse. Sometimes you need to double-click to open a computer file.

Downloading. This is to take something down from the internet into your computer. You can download documents, computer files, video files, and so on; it is the opposite of **uploading** your information onto the internet. Downloading is "to receive data from a remote system, such as a website, server, or other similar systems. The term is often applied to the massive retrieval of music, DVD movies, software, and more. This usage is correct as long as the data is being received."

Drop-down menu or **drop-down list**. Sometimes a MySpace page will have a box with an arrow pointing down to the side of the box. If you click on that arrow a menu or list of options will drop down. You can then point and click to choose the one that best suits your needs.

DSL. For our purposes DSL is a way to connect to the internet that lets information be processed much faster than using a dial-up internet connection. It allows for your family to receive phone calls while someone is **online** and allows for speedy transmission of pictures, music, videos, and most of the cool features on MySpace.

Technically speaking, DSL is "broadband digital communications connection that operates over standard copper telephone wires. It requires a DSL modem, which splits transmissions into two frequency bands: the lower frequencies for voice (ordinary telephone calls) and the upper band for digital data, especially for connection to the Internet. Data can be transferred via DSL at much higher rates than with ordinary dial-up modem service." This is also called a high-speed internet connection.

Email. Electronic mail, messages sent electronically by computers via the internet. MySpace and most social networking sites have email available; there are many other email providers who will allow users to set up email accounts for free or for a monthly fee.

Email address. If you are going to send mail electronically, you have to create an email address that will have some name, followed by @ (which means "at"), followed by the name of the email service provider. MySpace requires a separate email address for each profile. A person can have as many MySpace pages as they have email addresses. "A system for sending and receiving messages electronically over a computer network, as between personal computers; a message or messages sent or received by such a system."

Extended network (MySpace). On MySpace you will assemble your list of "friends." Each of your designated friends on MySpace has their list of friends on their MySpace page. Your list of friends on MySpace makes up your primary network; your extended network includes your friends, their friends, and all the friends of friends of friends. A personal profile page on MySpace displays the number of pages in that profile's extended network.

FAQ. Frequently asked questions.

Forums. Traditionally a forum has been a public gathering where discussion is to take place. **Online** forums are a gathering of people meeting via the internet using their computers to voice their discussions by typing on their keyboards. Online forums usually are divided into specific groups or topics. When a person chooses a topic from forum discussion selections and follows the directions to participate in that forum (usually by clicking on the topic), they are taken to a screen where the discussion is taking place in real time. This screen where the discussion is taking place is called the **chat room**.

Generation X. The generation following the post-World War II Baby Boom generation, especially people born in the United States and Canada from the early 1960s to the late 1970s.

Hand-held wireless device. This is a small portable device that works without wires. This can be a device that allows the user to use email, phone, text messaging, Web browsing, organizer (calendar, addresses, tasks, etc.), as well as paging, instant messaging, and data access — all from an electronic device that can be held in your hand. These include cell phones, BlackBerry devices, palm pilots, pocket PCs (personal computers), and Helios (which are used to go on MySpace).

Home page. "The main page of a World Wide Web site or the page where an individual Web browser is set, as the first viewed page when the browser starts up."

Home page for MySpace. When you go to *www.MySpace.com*, you will be taken to the home page for MySpace in general. This is not anyone's profile page; rather, it is the "virtual visitor's center" for MySpace. From the MySpace home page members can log in or new people can sign up to become a member. This is also where many other features of MySpace can be accessed by nonmembers who are checking it out.

Home page for a profile on MySpace. Each MySpace member has a personal profile page that has its own home page. This includes the default photo, user name, headline, and basic information. If the profile is public, their blogs, pics, videos, and so on can be accessed from the home page of the personal profile. You can also access a home page for a personal profile if you know their **URL** by typing it into the address line of your browser. For example, the home page for my profile on MySpace for this book is found at *www.myspace.com/momsanddads*. Other social networking sites work the same way: Xanga users can find my home page for this profile at *www.Xanga.com/dadsandmoms*, or Xianz users can find it at *www.Xianz.com/momsanddads*.

HTML. Sometimes you will see something that says "HTML" or "No HTML." HTML stands for Hyper-Text Markup Language. For our purposes it simply means the system used to set up hyperlinks between web pages. See **hyperlink** for more.

Hyperlink. Sometimes you will see words on a web page that are highlighted or highlighted and underlined. These are usually hyperlinks that link the web page you are on to the web page associated with that word. For example, if you go to the Safety Tips or Tips for Parents on MySpace.com, you will see a list of cyber-safety organizations, each one highlighted. If you click on any of these, your computer will take you to their page, which has been linked to the page from which you came.

This technology makes it easy for you to go from point of interest to point of interest without having to type in new addresses. The computer language used to make this work is referred to as **HTML**. A hyperlink is "an icon, graphic, or word in a file that, when clicked with the mouse, opens another file for viewing or takes the user to another location in the file. Web Pages often include hyperlinks (often called simply Links) to other pages at the same or another website."

ID. A term that means "identification." When you **log in** to certain websites as a member (such as MySpace), you usually have to give a member ID (or user name) and a password.

IM (Instant Messaging). This is sending a text message instantly to someone else who is also connected to the internet. MySpace has IM options, but teens also use IM outside of MySpace on their personal computers, cell phones, and other electronic devices. Think of this sort of like passing notes without using paper.

Internet. An interconnected network of computers. The internet worldwide is known as the World Wide Web. This network metaphorically resembles a spider web in design, so it's like a web of interconnected strands of communication around the world.

Internet browser. Since the internet is so vast and worldwide, people need help finding what they are looking for on the internet. Services are provided to help you browse the internet, looking for what you need. The most popular currently are Yahoo (*www.yahoo.com*), Google (*www.google.com*), and America Online (*www.aol.com*).

Internet browser address bar. A URL bar, or location bar/address bar, is a widget in a web browser that indicates the URL of the web page currently viewed. A new page can be viewed by typing its URL to the URL bar.

Kudos. "Praise, acclaim; an expression of warm approval." MySpace allows for kudos on the blogs, music, and pics. If we see something we like on our teen's page, we should be sure to leave them kudos!

Links. Various web pages set up links to other pages with useful information. The links are the text or graphics that serve as the point of reference to take you to the related page. "A segment of text or a graphical item that serves as a cross-reference between parts of a hypertext document or between files or hypertext documents; also called *hotlink, hyperlink*."

Login or log in. "The process of gaining access, or signing in, to a computer system. The process (the noun) is a 'logon' or 'login,' while the act of doing it (the verb) is to 'log on' or 'log in.' If access is restricted, the logon requires users to identify themselves by entering an **ID** number and/or password."

Member login box. To get into MySpace (and other internet sites) you may need to "log in" or "log on" to the service. This is usually done by typing in information such as your user name and password. On the MySpace **home page** there is a box where members can log in, usually found in the top right quadrant of that page.

Menu bar. "A horizontal strip near the top of the screen or a window, containing the titles of available pull-down menus."

Message board. A message board in computer terms is a computer system that lets users, usually associated in a designated group, post information or share software and information by adding theirs to what is already posted. This is often called a "bulletin board," but don't confuse this with sending a **bulletin** on MySpace. When you send a bulletin, you are sending multiple copies of one message to many people. When you post something on a bulletin board or message board, you are adding your single post to a board where many people can find it if they are looking for that topic.

Millennial generation. The last generation of people born in the twentieth century, also called Generation Y.

Moderator. A moderator is someone who oversees and arbitrates during a public forum, debate, or discussion. Some social networking sites, forums, and chat rooms use a moderator to keep the discussion on track and to monitor any users who may be getting out of line. A moderator usually has the power to ignore or block anyone they deem disruptive to the purpose of the forum. On MySpace many forum chat rooms do not have a moderator. Each school group set up through MySpace Schools seeks to have a moderator, and you should be able to find your teen's school's moderator and be added to his or her friends list. This may help you keep up to date with happenings at your teen's school. A forum or chat room with a moderator is usually somewhat safer than those without.

Monitoring software. Monitoring software is a computer program that allows someone to monitor the activity on their computer to various degrees. MySpace Tips for Parents usually has hyperlinks to monitoring software providers.

Mood icons. "Small pictograms used to indicate an emotion or attitude." These are sometimes available to add to a blog or other social networking posts. There is a drop-down list of moods from which to choose; with teens these can change frequently ☺.

Mosaics or Mosaic Generation. This refers to the generation of people who have grown up with the internet and therefore are more comfortable processing information that comes to them in the form of a mosaic rather than in linear form. According to Wikipedia, "the Mosaic Generation is a term used to describe those born between 1984 and 2002. The term was coined by Christian author George Barna and is mainly used within Evangelical Christian circles — most sources refer to this generation by the name 'Generation Y' or 'iGeneration.'" According to Barna, this generation is "very mosaic in every aspect of their life." He continues, "There's [no attribute] that really dominates like you might have seen with prior generations." Barna also describes this group as "comfortable with contradiction," "post-modern," and exhibiting "non-linear" thinking.

Mouse. A pointing device used to move the cursor on a computer screen so you can indicate what action you want the computer to take when you use the mouse to "point and click." The mouse comes in various forms but usually has buttons on the left and right that you can click. (See **click** for more information.) "The most popular hand-held pointing device, designed to sit under one hand of the computer user and to detect movement relative to its two-dimensional supporting surface. In addition, it usually features buttons and/or other devices, such as 'wheels,' which allow the user to perform various system-dependent operations. Extra buttons or features can add more control or dimensional input."

NCMEC CyberTipline. NCMEC stands for the National Center for Missing and Exploited Children. Their website explains: "The Congressionally mandated CyberTipline is a reporting mechanism for cases of child sexual exploitation including child pornography, online enticement of children for sex acts, molestation of children outside the family, sex tourism of children, child victims of prostitution, and unsolicited obscene material sent to a child. Reports may be made 24-hours per day, 7 days per week online at *www.cybertipline.com* or by calling 1-800-843-5678.

Online. To be "online" is to be accessible by computer via the internet. On MySpace there is a feature that allows users to have their page say "Online now" if they are using the computer. This allows others to know if they are available for Instant Messaging. You can use your account settings and privacy settings to hide the "Online now" alert.

Password. A selection of secret letters, numbers, and symbols used to allow only the user to gain access to their MySpace account or other internet pages that require a password. This protects the user and user's confidential information; therefore, passwords should be kept secret. In order to enhance security, passwords should be changed periodically.

Phishing or phishing scam. Pronounced "fishing," think of this as a fishing expedition where scammers and con artists are trying to trick someone into giving them valuable personal information they can use to rip people off in various ways. A common phishing scam will be a pop up ad or email saying it is from a website you trust (maybe eBay or MySpace or your bank), telling you that your information or password has been compromised, and if you don't give them the information your account will be closed. Bottom line, *never* give personal information such as your password, social security number, real name, or financial information to anyone who contacts you.

If you think it might be legitimate, get out of the program where you were contacted, go to your own **internet browser**, go to the website you trust, and check with them.

Podcasts. Short for "iPod broadcast." An audio broadcast that has been converted to an MP3 file or other audio file format for playback in a digital music player or computer." Through MySpace users can arrange to send out their content as a podcast.

Pics. Short for pictures or photos on MySpace.

Profile design. This is the way your web page or MySpace profile looks. There are countless ways a user can design a profile, including various colors, animation, slide shows, photos, sounds, music, and design elements. To many teens designing their MySpace page has become as important or more important than decorating their room.

Public forum. See **forums.**

Right click. (See **click.**) "Right click" means to press the button on the right side of your **mouse** to get other options than clicking or pressing the left button of the mouse.

Screen shot or screen capture. This is to capture and save what you see in one screen of a website; it's like taking a photographic "shot" of what's on the page at that moment. Some keyboards have a button that says "Print Screen" to make this easier. "Transferring the current on-screen image to a text or graphics file. There is a 'Print Screen' function in the operating system that copies the contents of the active window to the clipboard, which can then be pasted into a graphics application to print it. If there is no active window, the entire desktop is copied."

Scroll (verb). Just as ancient scrolls needed to be rolled through to find what one wanted to read, so too computer pages can be rolled up or down to find what you are looking for; this action of rolling the page up or down is called scrolling. You may be told to scroll to the top or bottom of a page; to do so you can use the up and down arrows usually found to the right of the page, or your **mouse** may have a special way you can use the device to scroll without using the arrows. "To move up and down (or from side to side) in a computer file, bringing different information into view, as if the computer screen were the visible portion of a scroll being unrolled at one end and rolled up at the other."

Search bar. On MySpace there is a bar at the top of the MySpace home page used to search for various things. This is the search bar for MySpace. Many websites include a search bar consisting of a space where you can type in a key word related to what you are looking for on that site and click on the "go" or "search" button to find your choice.

Social networking. This term can be used for in-person, face-to-face social networking, meeting people and getting to know them, interacting so-cially. It is also a term used to describe connecting with people socially through the internet.

Social networking site. A site on the internet used for social networking. This includes MySpace, Xianz, Xanga, Facebook, Bebo, Friendster, MeetFish, and hundreds of others.

Software. The solid and tangible parts of your computer are known as "hard-ware"; the programs that determine what your computer does or the brains of the operation are known as the software.

Spyware. Computer software is "a type of program that watches what users are doing with their computer and then sends that information over the internet. Spyware can collect many different types of information about a user. More benign programs can attempt to track what types of websites a user visits and send this information to an advertisement agency. More malicious versions can try to record what a user types to try to intercept passwords or credit card numbers. Yet other versions simply launch popup advertisements."

Some parents use spyware to see where their teens are going online; spouses may use spyware to see what the other spouse is doing online; some employers use it to check up on their employees. Using spyware will get you information, but if discovered it will seriously undermine trust. Think seriously about the possible ramifications of using it. Also, many teens know how to get around it, so you could jeopardize your relationship without accomplishing your aim.

Surfer or surfing (the Web). As a surfer on the ocean waves goes from one to another, not knowing what's coming next, so too a person can go casually from one website to another on the internet, allowing one wave of infor-mation to lead them to the next. This is known as surfing the web; those who do it are known as web surfers.

Techies. People who are so comfortable with technology that they have earned a nickname all their own.

Toolbar. A computer toolbar is a bar, usually across the top but it can be in other configurations, that have tools to make computer use or the naviga-tion of a website easier. The toolbar usually has icons or visual images to represent what that tool will help you do. For example, the "spell check" tool on a word processing program may be represented by the letters ABC in the icon; the "print" function may be represented by an image of a printer.

Trick out. "Ornament or adorn, especially ostentatiously or garishly." Some teens get very involved in learning to "trick out" their MySpace profile. While doing so they learn computer and design skills.

Uploading. This is the process by which a person takes some information or media they have and put it *up* on the internet. It is the opposite of **downloading**, where a person takes something down from the internet into their website or computer.

URL. This stands for Uniform Resource Locator—in other words, a **website address**.

Username. "The name you use to identify yourself when logging onto a computer system or online service. Both a username (user **ID**) and a **password** are required. In an internet email address, the username is the left part before the @ sign. For example, karenb is the username in **karenb@my-company.com**."

Web 2.0. Simply speaking, this refers to the second level of internet use. When the internet first began to be used by the general public, it was used primarily as a *source* of information. People went to a website to find something that was already there and to view or retrieve the information. The second level of internet use came when technology changed to become so easy to use and computer connections became so fast that many people with computers could just as easily *contribute* their content *to* the web as get information *from* the web.

The definition of Web 2.0 is still being formed, and various computer experts give specific definitions, but this general one serves our purposes. Before "Web 2.0" your teens would not have been able to make their MySpace profile and post it to the internet. Now that they can, it becomes an issue about which parents need to become informed. "Sometimes called the 'New Internet,' Web 2.0 is not a specific technology; rather, it encompasses blogs, **Wikis** and online communities such as Friendster, MySpace and Facebook. Web 2.0 implies social change with user-generated content being a major driving force."

Web browser. Same as **Internet browser** (see definition).

Web Log or Weblog. A log, journal, or commentary kept on a website. Some people have merged the words web log into one word (i.e., weblog). This was shortened to become the commonly used word **blog**. MySpace and other social networking sites make keeping up a web log easy so it has become more popular among teens. If your teen keeps a blog on MySpace, you can subscribe to it and receive notices when a new entry is posted. "A website that displays in chronological order the postings by one or more individuals and usually has links to comments on specific postings."

Website. A Web site or website is a particular place on the internet or "web" of interconnected computers. The website usually has an assortment of information and images collected and maintained by the person, group, or organization in charge of that site. Each website will have a **home page** that will lead you to the rest of the pages associated with that site and may have links to other websites recommended by the original site. Website is a general term, a MySpace profile can be considered a website, but people have websites outside of MySpace.

Website address. Each website has an address that will take you to that place on the Web. This address often begins with www. (which stands for the World Wide Web), then a descriptive series of letters or letters and numbers/symbols, followed by .com (for commercial- oriented purposes), .org (for nonprofit organizations), .net (for internet providers), .gov (for government sites), or .edu (for educational sites). I have a Web address for my personal website, mostly used for archiving passed articles, interviews about Harry Potter, and various books I've written at *www.ConnieNeal.com*. I also have website addresses for the social networking related pages I have created to accompany this book. See **Home page for profile on MySpace** in this glossary, where I have listed the website addresses for each of my MySpace profiles. The website address is also called the **URL**.

Wikis. *Wiki wiki* is Hawaiian for "quick." Internet communities where users can add or edit information so that it is quickly and continually changing are called wikis. An example is Wikipedia (*www.wikipedia.org*), where the encyclopedia-type articles and definitions are continually being changed, checked, and updated by users.

Wikipedia. Made up of the words "wiki" (Hawaiian for "quick") and "encyclopedia," this is an online encyclopedia that is always evolving and always being edited and verified by contributors all over the world.

World Wide Web. A descriptive term for the internet or interconnected network of computers that operates all around the world, abbreviated as www or the "Web."

www. This abbreviations stands for World Wide Web (see **Internet**).

Cyber-Safety Organizations and Resources

The organizations listed here are those of good reputation that are committed to maintaining and distributing information and resources to help you make sure your teens and kids are safe online. Since websites are continually changing, I tried to give additional information as well as the Web address. Note that the websites and addresses may change. So even if the Web addresses change, these long-standing organizations should still be operating. You can call the phone number or find them by using a Web browser or search engine to track down the latest information.

Since some readers of this book are more comfortable using the telephone or mail to a street address than they are using the internet and email, I have included that information whenever it was available. When it was not available I gave the Web address so you could locate their information on the internet. When looking for a Web address, be careful to make sure you have the right ending such as .com, .org, .net, .gov, or .edu, because a different ending or a dot (".") out of place can take you to an entirely different site.

Since these sites are continually changing and updating, I'll let you contact them to learn more about them and what they have to offer for yourself. Also remember that you will be able to find up-to-date cyber safety information on the Safety Tips and Tips for Parents pages of MySpace. Here I only included organizations that have earned a good reputation and my trust. If you start with these, you should have access to plenty of reliable and helpful information.

BlogSafety.com (affiliated with SafeTeens.com and NetFamilyNews.org)
Run by Larry Magid and Anne Collier
Street Address: 706 Colorado Ave. Palo Alto, CA 94303
Web Address: *www.BlogSafety.com*

California Cyber Safety Summit
California Department of Consumer Affairs
Email Address: CyberSafety@dca.ca.gov
Web Address: *www.cybersafety.ca.gov/*

Common Sense Media
Street Address: Common Sense Media, 1550 Bryant Street, Suite 555,
   San Francisco, CA 94103
Phone: 415-863-0600
Web Address: *www.CommonSenseMedia.org*

Federal Bureau of Investigation: A Parent's Guide to Internet Safety
Street Address: Federal Bureau of Investigation, Cyber Division, Innocent
   Images National Initiative, 11700 Beltsville Drive, Calverton, MD 20705
Web Address: *www.fbi.gov/publications/pguide/pguidee.htm*
For further information, please contact your local FBI office or the National
   Center for Missing and Exploited Children.

Focus on the Family Internet Safety Links
Street Address: Focus on the Family, Colorado Springs, CO 80995
Web Address: *www.focusonyourchild.com/hottopics/A0001282.cfm*
Phone: 1-800-A-FAMILY (1-800-232-6459)

The National Center for Missing and Exploited Children
The NCMEC maintains a 24-hour multilingual hotline at 1-800-THE-
   LOST (1-800-843-5678) and a website at *www.missingkids.com* to
   provide:

- assistance to parents and law enforcement agencies about missing or
  sexually exploited chidren
- a central location to receive reports of missing children sightings
- parents with information on how to better safeguard their children
- reunification assistance to parents once their children are found.

NCMEC operates a CyberTipline at *www.cybertipline.com* that allows
   parents and children to report child pornography and sexual exploitation
   of children by submitting an online form. This form is then reviewed by
   analysts and forwarded to law enforcement including the FBI, the U.S.

Customs Service, the U.S. Postal Inspection Service, and state and local police agencies.

NetSmartz
Street Address: Charles B. Wang International Children's Building, 699 Prince Street, Alexandria, VA 22314–3175
Phone: 1-800-THE-LOST (1-800-843-5678)
Web Address: *www.netsmartz.org/*
The NetSmartz Workshop is an interactive, educational safety resource from the National Center for Missing & Exploited Children® (NCMEC) and Boys & Girls Clubs of America (BGCA) for children aged 5 to 17, parents, guardians, educators, and law enforcement that uses age-appropriate, 3-D activities to teach children how to stay safer on the internet.

ProtectKids.com (sister site to Enough is Enough at *www.enough.org*)
President: Donna Rice Hughes
Street Address: c/o Enough is Enough, 746 Walker Road, Suite 116, Great Falls, VA 22066
Phone: 1-888-744-0004 (Fax: 1-571-333-5685)
Web Address: *www.ProtectKids.com*

Web Wise Kids
Mail address: P.O. Box 27203, Santa Ana, CA 92799
Phone: 1-866-WEB-WISE (1-866-932-9473); Fax: 1-714-435-0523
Email: info@webwisekids.org
Web address: *www.wiredwithwisdom.org*
To order the video game *Missing,* call 1-714-435-2885 or 1-866-WEB-WISE.

WiredSafety.org
Executive Director: Parry Aftab, Esq.
Web Address: *www.wiredsafety.org*
Email Address: askParry@wiredsafety.org

Books and Other Resources

These books and resources will either help you learn more about how to keep your teens safe online or help you with issues that may arise when you get to know more about their lives through your exploration of social networking. Some of the problems blamed on MySpace are actually *revealed by* MySpace. If you run across problems in your exploration of MySpace, check these resources or books (most available at *www.amazon.com*, which is a trustworthy internet bookseller). Hopefully you will find something that addresses the needs that arise for you. All you really need to know to find these books online or through your local bookseller is the title and author. When more information was available I supplied it below.

Bullying

No More Victims, by Frank Peretti

Cyberbullying and Cyberthreats: Responding to the Challenge of Online Social Cruelty, Threats, and Distress, by Nancy E. Willard

Emerging Sexuality

Preparing for Adolescence: How to Survive the Coming Years of Change, by James C. Dobson

Every Young Man's Battle: Strategies for Victory in the Real World of Sexual Temptation, by Stephen Arterburn and Fred Stoeker with Mike Yorkey

Every Young Woman's Battle: Guarding Your Mind, Heart, and Body in a Sex-Saturated World, by Shannon Ethridge and Stephen Arterburn

Preparing Your Daughter for Every Woman's Battle: *Creative Conversations about Sexual and Emotional Integrity*, by Shannon Ethridge and Stephen Arterburn

Pornography

Questions and answers along with articles related to dealing with pornography can be found at *www.family.org/married/topics/a0025117.cfm*
Focus on the Family
Colorado Springs, CO 80995
1-800-A-FAMILY (232-6459)

Every Young Man's Battle: *Strategies for Victory in the Real World of Sexual Temptation*, by Stephen Arterburn and Fred Stoeker with Mike Yorkey

Help! Someone I Know Has a Problem with Porn, by Bill Maier and Jim Vigorito

Breaking Free: *Understanding Sexual Addiction & the Healing Power of Jesus*, by Russell Willingham

Confidence and Self-Esteem

The New Hide or Seek: *Building Confidence in Your Child*, by James C. Dobson

Raising Positive Kids in a Negative World, by Zig Ziglar

How Am I Smart? A Parent's Guide to Multiple Intelligences, by Dr. Kathy Koch

Parenting and Parent-Teen Relationships

Kathy Koch, PhD, the founder and president of Celebrate Kids, Inc., is a dynamic presenter to teens, parents, and educators. In addition to her live programs, her two books provide important insights: *Finding Authentic Hope and Wholeness*: *5 Questions that Will Change Your Life*, and *How Am I Smart? A Parent's Guide to Multiple Intelligences* (2007). Celebrate Kids has produced public school versions of both of these books as DVDs. I highly recommend them: *Life Changing Questions*: *Authentic Answers*, and *How Am I Smart? A Guide to Multiple Intelligences*. These and other helpful information and resources are available from her website *www.CelebrateKids.com* or by calling 1-817-238-2020.

Walking Tall in Babylon: *Raising Children to Be Godly and Wise in a Perilous World*, by Connie Neal

Preparing for Adolescence: *How to Survive the Coming Years of Change*, by James C. Dobson

The DNA of Parent-Teen Relationships: *Discover the Key to Your Teen's Heart*, by Gary Smalley and Greg Smalley

Age of Opportunity: *A Biblical Guide to Parenting Teens*, by Paul David Tripp

Bringing Up Boys, by James C. Dobson

Books about MySpace and Cyber Safety

MySpace Unraveled, by Larry Magid and Anne Collier

MySpace Visual Quick Tips, by Sherry Willard Kinkoph and Paul McFedries

Cyber-Safe Kids, Cyber-Savvy Teens: *Helping Young People Learn to Use the Internet Safely and Responsibly*, by Nancy E. Willard

Kids Online, by Donna Rice Hughes

Notes

Notes

Notes

Notes

Notes

Notes

Notes

Notes

Notes

Dancing in the Arms of God

Finding Intimacy and Fulfillment by Following His Lead

Connie Neal

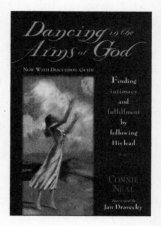

Deep within, every woman longs for her own Cinderella experience: to rise from her humble past, discover the best in herself, and be appreciated by a true, lasting love. Yet, her own efforts to fill the yearning often end in tatters. And no man can rescue her. In *Dancing in the Arms of God*, the Cinderella fairy tale provides a powerful allegory for women's deepest hopes and dreams and the God who longs to fill them. It's a message proved true in the life of author Connie Neal. For all of us who have wrestled with disillusionment, abandonment, our own limitations, and the lies that whisper we're not beautiful, Connie's true-life insights reveal what it means to dance with God . . . following his lead until every promise he's ever made proves true.

Softcover 0-310-21915-9

Pick up a copy today at your favorite bookstore!

We want to hear from you. Please send your comments about this book to us in care of zreview@zondervan.com. Thank you.

ZONDERVAN.com/
AUTHORTRACKER
follow your favorite authors